ACHIEVER'S ZO

Achiever's Zone is a n
training organization
training to various verticals across all sectors. It is headquartered in Singapore and has multi-country presence.

It specializes in entrepreneur development, leadership development, people skills and effective grooming. We are capable of providing corporate training to meet different needs; diagnostic services for organizations; design, develop and execution of customized training solution keeping in mind different organizational goals.

We are a company dedicated to performance enhancement and work towards developing high performance teams with end-to-end solutions approach. We also undertake large initiatives across the country towards development of fresh talents with soft skills, necessary grooming to improve their job readiness, thereby improving the overall employability factor in the country. Our endeavour is to offer best value solutions with an integrated learning approach and a continued on-going support to the team.

As India is poised for unbelievable growth in almost every sector, our motto is to help our clients to rise up to the upcoming opportunities by providing right training to the people who matter the most.

To know more about Achievers Zone please log on to www.achieverszone.com

ACHIEVERS ZONE

Live Your Best Life Now

Live Your Best Life Now

Live, Love, and Laugh Full Out

Sean Willard

"From the first page through to the last paragraph, I was captivated by Sean Willard's inspiring and engaging wisdom. As you read this book, be prepared to have your life transformed in truly positive ways. You may want to consider getting a copy of *Live Your Best Life Now* for those you love and deeply care about. I'm certain they'll be thrilled you did."

—Peggy McColl, New York Times Bestselling Author

EBD

Embassy Books

This edition published in India 2012.

Published in India by :
EMBASSY BOOK DISTRIBUTORS
120, Great Western Building,
Maharashtra Chamber of Commerce Lane,
Fort, Mumbai - 400 023.
Tel : (+91-22) 22819546 / 32967415
Email : info@embassybooks.in
Website: www.embassybooks.in

ISBN : 978-93-81860-13-7

Printed and Bound in India by
Repro India Ltd., Navi Mumbai

In loving memory of my dad and hero,
Les Willard—miss our chats!

Acknowledgments:

I am learning that possibly the most difficult section of a book to write is the page where you get to thank and acknowledge individuals for their incredible input into your authoring journey.

I run the risk of omitting someone special from this section, and if you know me, you will know that that is the last thing I would ever want to do!

So, to all you wonderful people out there who have encouraged me to press through and urged me to live my Purpose *On Purpose*—a huge THANK YOU!

Special mention must go to my beautiful wife, Michele, who has patiently supported and believed in me over twenty-five years of friendship and twenty years of incredible marriage. I am blessed beyond words to have you in my life!

Nathan and Tegan, I cherish your hearts of love and times of laughter shared with you each and every day.

To my mom, June—thank you for the example of love you have set for your family—I love you!

To my sister, Colleen—it is impossible to put into words just how much you mean to me. You are a gift from heaven!

To my brother, Dave—your belief in me has meant the world to me. Thank you!

Special thanks to Jean Morrissey—This journey and your gifting and ability to weave my thoughts and words into a story that needed to be shared has been beyond special. Thank you for Living your Purpose!

To the coaches and mentors who have influenced my journey to date: Les Brown, Paul Martinelli, Bob Proctor, Sandy Griffin, Peggy McColl, John Maxwell and John Sheasby (among many, many others)—thank you!

To my Father, whose grace is all I need. Thank You!

Contents

I could not breathe!

"Wake up, Sean. *Wake up*!" My brain urgently admonished my disorientated and sleepy body.

It took a few seconds for me to register that this was no nightmare. It was *real*. And I was in trouble ...

INTRODUCTION

Are You *On* Purpose?

"Life loves the liver of it."

Maya Angelou

There is nothing quite like the feeling of taking life by the horns, staring it in the eyeball, and willing it do what you want it to do.

It is similar to the sensation you get during a rugby match after smashing an opponent into the ground "boots an' all," or after taking a piece of clay, wire, or fabric and successfully molding it to the shape you desire.

In both instances, you have plotted a particular course, decided on the outcome, and then tried your hardest to bring that outcome into reality.

The attempt, followed by a measure of success, is extremely rewarding.

Although many of us know how to plan or dream on a small scale to achieve results in our lives, the truth is that very few of us have been taught or have learned the art of living *every* aspect of our lives *on Purpose.*

To live one's life *on Purpose* is, quite simply, to not live it by mistake. To live one's life *on Purpose* is to have a rudder on one's Life Boat,[1] supplies in the cabin, and a direction in which you are *specifically* headed for a *specific* reason that is specifically *yours.*

1 Your metaphorical boat that you use to navigate life; *not* a small rubber boat you use to escape from a sinking ship…

Living *on Purpose* is living on course—with your daily activities and actions working in congruence with your passions, dreams, and vision for your life.

To live one's life by mistake, on the other hand, is to bob around in your Life Boat with no rudder, no supplies, and possibly no cabin—leaving the outcome largely up to fate, wishful thinking, other people, and external influences, all mixed in with a sizeable measure of good luck.

When you land on islands and reefs that you had no intention of reaching, feeling bored, hollow, under-utilized, disillusioned, frustrated, and possibly wet, you wonder how it can be so.

You watch others whizzing past with grins on their faces, the wind of success in their sails, and you feel jealous.

The truth is that you are *off* course to your dreams and life vision. You have been living by *mistake*.

As I coach and speak to people around the country, I ask them the following pressing question: WHAT IS YOUR PURPOSE? About 95 percent of the people I meet do not have the foggiest idea and usually answer my question with a blank stare!

They do not know the *why* of their existence, and because they do not know their *why,* they may live with feelings of insignificance, frustration, and a nagging sense that things are not quite as they should be. This is tragic!

If you are one of these 95 percent who are still paddling in circles, uncertain of the direction you should take in life and the reason you should take it, I urge you to read on.

My hope is that as we journey through the pages of this book together, you will allow me to come alongside you on your journey of discovering your *why* and that this will bring about change and purposeful living.

Your ingrained potential is just bursting at the seams to be recognized and released. Your purpose preceded your person and is crying out to be appreciated and lived into!

It might need some dusting and polishing; it might be buried deep under a forgotten box somewhere on your Life Boat, right next door to your hopes and dreams; it might surprise you immensely when you finally find it; it is there, waiting for discovery, acknowledgement, and a good workout.

The Life Attack Challenge is a process of discovery that we all must journey on if we truly want to live *full* lives!

Are you ready?

Sean's Story

"If the ladder is not leaning against the right wall, every step we take just gets us to the wrong place faster."

—Stephen R. Covey

I was a pharmacist for over nineteen years of my life before I set sail on my own Life Attack journey.

I am a highly energized, fun-loving, extroverted, make-it-happen kind of guy who loves his family a great deal and who has always loved people. I love encouraging, motivating, and putting a smile on someone's dial.

I am the guy in his Life Boat who shouts happily to others as they row or sail on by—even if they find it startling or annoying!

I can confidently say that I know how I *tick.*

Although my work as a pharmacist brought me into contact with plenty of people with whom to connect, laugh and encourage, I always had a niggling feeling that while I should be doing all of that (it just comes naturally to me), I was not in the right place doing it.

I had chosen the wrong arena in which to live out my life purpose.

This I already knew by my second year of pharmaceutical studies. The reasons I chose this career path are vague and may even have included a casual conversation with a good friend and an old girlfriend. (Boys will be boys!) Vagueness, however, is not a good driving force for any future.

Since what I was studying did not seem to "fit," I took a week off in my second year to try to find myself and figure out an alternative life plan. This resulted in a very distressed and desperate plea from my family to at least push through until year end—which I did!

By then, the ball was rolling at a pace, and I never jumped off. So a pharmacist I became and a pharmacist I stayed for many years.

There is a hilarious scene in the comedy movie *Little Miss Sunshine* where a family, racing against the clock to get their daughter/sister/grandchild/niece to a specific venue in time for her to enter a beauty pageant, takes a turn off the freeway at what seems to be the obvious exit—with their destination standing directly ahead of them—only to find that the route they have chosen swings them enticingly close and then around and away from where they need to be.

You can imagine the shouts of dismay that erupt in the van as they realize what is happening and the frantic plan of action that follows to correct this error.

As a young man, with my family's firm encouragement, I took a wrong career "exit"—somehow thinking that irrespective of heading off in a direction opposite to my dreams, I would still land up where I truly wanted to be in life.

"If the ladder is not leaning against the right wall, every step we take just gets us to the wrong place faster," says Stephen R. Covey.

I had taken my life/"ladder," propped it against the "wall" of a future in pharmacy, and found that even though every step I took on my life journey as a pharmacist did take me higher, it never took me on the path I wanted to be on.

If someone had sat me down as a young man and asked me to do some critical thinking about my passions, purpose, and goals in life, I would have probably managed to place my ladder against the correct wall a long time ago.[2]

Eventually, in 2008, I tucked my ladder under one arm, sold my pharmacy, and began to explore my true purpose and talents.

---

2 This is not to say that I believe that all those years were wasted. One of the key mistakes we make in goal-setting is believing that the process is only about "reaching the goal" when, in fact, *who we become* on the journey to achieving our goals is even more important. With this perspective in mind, I have made peace with what I had initially thought were nineteen years of "wasted time."

I wanted to answer the question of *why* I was alive. I not only wanted to discover what I could be but who I could be if I gave myself the chance to explore my purpose further.

"In Between"

People often say that when you intentionally close one door in life, then another one automatically swings open for you to walk through.

This was not my experience at all!

The best way I can describe what happened to me is to use the analogy of a visit to my local bank.

To physically get in and out of my bank, I have to open a door, step into a small space, and wait for that door to seal shut behind me, which essentially leaves me standing, trapped in a vacuum, until a red light above the sealed door in front of me blinks to green. At this point, I am released to move on.

For a closet claustrophobic like me, the two-to-three-second delay in that "in-between" space is an uncomfortable sensation.

What if I do not get the green light to move on? What if the door jams shut and refuses to open due to a technical failure? How long will I then be stuck in that space, like a fish in a fishbowl?

When I sold my pharmacy, I pulled open a door, shut it behind me, and stepped into a vacuum.

I began to look around expectantly to see what new opportunities my bold choices would open up for me, but no light flashed to green above a door in front of me, and nothing significant came to pass.

It is easy in that "delay period" to begin to panic and feel as if you have missed it. All the "what ifs" begin to rise uncomfortably in your heart. What if no door will open for me? What if I will *never* step into my purpose?

I was in limbo like this, with life just happening to me, for several months. I even uprooted my family and moved them back to my home town of Port Elizabeth (PE) to explore some new, exciting vocational avenues.

It was while living in PE, on a visit back to our previous port of stay, Cape Town, that I was rudely woken one morning, feeling sleepy and disorientated in my sister and brother-in-law's guest room, fighting for breath!

There's nothing quite like an early-morning reflux asthma attack[3] to put one's life into proper perspective.

As I stood, bent double alongside the bed, with my hands on my knees, sucking and gasping for air so loudly that Sandy and her husband, Norman, were soon awake and rushing into the room to join me, I felt helpless and doomed. I remember thinking to myself, "You are only forty years old!"

With two pairs of anxious eyes watching, I felt myself begin to fade. I kept thinking, *This must be a dream—I must wake up!* until finally I realized … *this is it;* this is the real deal. And there was nothing I could do.

Suddenly, my airway popped open, and I could get in that much-needed breath of air … and breathe I did!

That experience lasted all of sixty seconds—but it has truly been one of the most defining minutes of my life.

The sheer panic that gripped me at the time crystallized and formalized itself into three of the most important questions I have ever asked myself:

Have I *really* LIVED, have I *really* LOVED, and have I *really* LAUGHED in life?

The answer was a resounding no. I knew that I want *more!*

---

3 According to doctors, an evening of good wining and dining like I'd had the night before, followed by some pre-bed biscuit-munching and a few hours of lying down, can lead to stomach acid build-up in the oesophagus.

The acid irritates the surrounding nerves and may also be aspirated into the trachea in small amounts, causing reflex closure of the trachea and lower airways. This is known as a reflux asthma attack.

The Chinese Bamboo Tree

As a "make-it-happen" kind of guy, I wish that I could tell you that after that incident two years ago, I began to suck as much of the delicious marrow out of life as I could.

I wish it were true that I began to live and love well, that I fully engaged myself in enjoying the journey along the way, and that I simply slipstreamed into living out my purpose.

A near-death experience should have completely altered me from the inside out, right?

Rather, I believe that an intellectual seed, an idea, to live and love and laugh well, was planted in my mind that breathless morning, and it has needed me to invite it into the right environment to help it grow.

Over these past two years, I have discovered just which life components (or ingredients) nurture this seed and which of these to steer clear of, in order to protect my seed from being stifled and starved.

Sometimes our daily choices can leave us knowing that we have encountered life in all its fullness, or alternatively, we can walk away feeling that we have just traded our dreams in for something unworthy of our time and energy.

I discovered that time spent with positive people who leave me feeling revived and energetic is good soil for intellectual seed growth, while gloomy and draining company often leaves my passions dampened and my creativity depressed.

I have had to take a look at the movies I watch, the books I read, the places I visit, and my own spiritual journey to assess how much of it was good or bad soil for seed growth.

I have gone about watering my intellectual seed by reading some challenging and thought-provoking material and by listening to a number of amazing speakers on similar subjects.

Rubbing shoulders with key people along the way has also been good soil for my seed's growth.

However, a seed *quietly* growing under the surface does not feel half as rewarding as one that is sending green shoots out from the soil—glorious evidence to the world that a full-blown Life Attack is underway.

I have definitely felt frustrated at the "below par" level of living, loving, and laughing that I have experienced.

I was reflecting upon this when I recalled the story of the Chinese Bamboo tree:[4]

> You take a little bamboo seed, plant it, water it, and fertilize it for a whole year…and nothing happens.
>
> The second year you water it, fertilize it … and nothing happens.
>
> The third year you water it, fertilize it … and (can you guess?) nothing happens.
>
> How discouraging this becomes!
>
> The fourth year you water it and fertilize it, and … *still* nothing happens. This is very frustrating.
>
> The fifth year you continue to water and fertilize the seed … and then sometime during the fifth year, the Chinese bamboo tree begins to sprout.
>
> It can now grow ninety feet in just six weeks!

Les Brown asks the question, "Did the tree grow ninety feet in three months or five years?!!"

We "instant gratification" types might be inclined to believe it took the tree three months to grow and that it simply wasted its time for those five long years.

The tree was *always* growing, irrespective of its apparent lack of production levels.

---

4 http://www.storiesofwisdom.com/a-lesson-from-the-chinese-bamboo-tree/

As we start off this journey together, I would like to encourage you, straight off the bat, not to get too impatient with yourself along the way. Never allow yourself to drop anchor in the waters of discouragement!

You clearly want change in your life. Why else would you be reading this book?

Change may not always appear in the package that you had hoped it would, and it might take longer than you expect it will, but it is a gift nonetheless; trust the process!

Sometimes "failure" that you experience will be a good opportunity for you to step out of the action to catch your breath, reflect, and make some honest appraisals.

Failure, after all, is just preparation, so get ready for lots of it. As John Maxwell says, we need to learn to "fail forwards."

Once you are back in the rhythm of your journey, you can hoist sails again and get on with attacking life the way you want to.

On Your Marks ...

So how are we going to Attack Life, you might ask?

Let us open the treasure chest and take out some tools that will help you have your very own Life Attack!

No two Life Attacks will ever be exactly the same, but my hope is that what I am learning and have learned from my own journey will spur you on and get you thinking and asking some vital questions.

Roll up your sleeves and be prepared to get dirty—it's Life Attack time!

THE LIFE ATTACK CHALLENGE:

Your Life Attack Tools

"Look, I don't want to wax philosophic, but I will say that if you're alive you've got to flap your arms and legs, you've got to jump around a lot, for life is the very opposite of death, and therefore you must at very least think noisy and colorfully, or you're not alive."

—Mel Brooks

Some time ago, I heard Wayne Dyer sharing a story that he had been given to read when he was a young man.

Wayne had been standing on a dock with his uncle Bill, waiting to embark on a twenty-nine-day journey across the Pacific Ocean in order to join the navy ship to which he had been assigned.

Wayne remembers that, as they said their farewells, Bill handed him a book of short stories by Leo Tolstoy and told him to specifically take a look at the one entitled, "The Death of Ivan Ilyich."

This story tells the tale of a judge in Moscow who hated his work, his wife, and much of everything about his life. He pursued this life regardless until, on his deathbed, he looked into his wife's eyes and asked her, "What if my whole life has been *wrong*?"

Then he died.

For Wayne, the message from this story was clear—choose to *live* life!

After reading the story, Wayne went on to journal himself a simple request: "Dear Wayne, don't die with your music still in you."

I believe that we can all make this request our own. In fact, "don't die with the music still in you" has already become one of my life aspirations and goals.

I don't want to reach my deathbed with all my potential and capacity still locked away inside me! Do you?

Reconciliation

Wayne's reference to the "music still in us" reminds me of the movie *August Rush,* which tells the story of a young boy with exceptional musical talents who leaves the orphanage in which he was raised in order to find his parents.

He believes that they are still alive, that his being put up for adoption was a mistake, that they still want him, and that if he "follows the music" in and around him, it will eventually lead him straight to his parents.

The music (passion) inside this boy draws him to encounter and affect numerous lives along the way and to be ultimately reconciled with his mom and dad.

I believe that once we answer the "music" (passion) inside our hearts, our purpose becomes reconciled with our vision, which leads us to achieve our goals and to live the life of our dreams.

We give birth, as such, to our goals when our passion causes our purpose and vision to unite.

I once heard someone sharing on purpose, visions, and goals describe purpose as being the *essence* of who you are, which serves as your "true north" for the decisions you make, the actions you take, and the results you achieve in your life.

This is why the first tool for your Life Attack Challenge is PASSION.

LIFE ATTACK TOOL #1: PASSION

Are you in love with your life? This is a vital question to ask yourself quite early in the game. If you are not leaping out of bed each morning, humming a happy, albeit off-key tune as you face the day ahead of you, then what exactly is the point, I ask you?

Do you merely exist to pay your dreaded bills?

Are you coasting through each minute of every single day until the weekend like a true thank-goodness-it's-Friday (TGIF) type of person? (If this is you, you'll be horrified to note that you hate 71.43% of your life at the moment!)

Are you aware that you are *allowed* to do what you love, because what you love to do is what you are meant to be doing with your life?

There are many possible reasons for your failure to pursue your passions and dreams:

- You might feel that you owe it to yourself, your parents, or your families to live "more responsibly"—pursuing sensible vocations that will provide a sensible income to secure yourself a sensible future.

  But all this sensibleness has you dozing in the audience of your own life. It's time to wake up!

> **It's time to "live your making," rather than make your living!**

- On occasion, you might have tumbled out of the nest in pursuit of those dreams whizzing by, only to be shot out of the sky with opinion and ridicule.

  Those holding the shotguns could have been your friends, parents, teachers, religious leaders, or other significant loved ones.

It is tough to be believed in less than we need to be. Consequently you may have chosen to walk everywhere and as a result have never learnt to fly.

Sadly, in the land of dreams, the biggest giants are often our closest friends and family.

- The concept of living and doing what you love might never have crossed your mind.

  You might have grown up believing that the things you love to do should be classified as hobbies and luxuries, while what you do for a living should taste, feel, and smell like work—arduous, boring, uninspiring, dutiful —definitely *not* like a kid let loose in the toy shop of his or her wildest imaginings!

- You might have bought into the belief that money or education is the deciding factor for living a life of dreaming.

  You long to live significantly and in step with your passions, but you just don't have the cash or the skills.

  You might have grown up hearing the sayings, "Money does not grow on trees"; "Who do you think I am, Rockefeller?"; or "Money talks—mine says good-bye!"

What Is Your Self-Talk about Money?

It might be comforting to know that Virgin's Richard Branson did not start his hugely successful life adventure with money or a tertiary education. He started with his talents and passions, around which he developed plans.

His firm conviction is that if you do what you enjoy and if you have fun while you are at it, the money will happen.[5]

---

5 Branson, Richard. 2006. *Screw It, Let's Do It: Lessons in Life.* Virgin Books, Great Britain. p. 13.

You *were never created to live a life of scarcity—you were created to live a life of abundance! The choice is yours—will you approach the ocean with a spoon, a cup, or a bucket? When you receive from abundance, there is always enough!*

- Sadly, the reality could be that *failure* is more daunting to you than sheer, life-sapping boredom.

  Instead of dreaming, you kit out your current *rut* of choice with a lean-to shack and settle for squatter rights instead of a trip on the Autobahn in your own Ferrari!

  You see, you had a Ferrari dream, but a VW Beetle paycheck ... the one with the double exhaust pipe, so that when you broke down, you could pick it up like a wheelbarrow and push it to the nearest garage. Your dreams and passions were downsized or capsized by the voices of "reason" around you ... even your own!

- Or, oddly enough, *success* (and therefore the pressure to continuously succeed) could be more daunting to you than any failure.

  You have boycotted yourself time and again—and have failed to find out how brilliant you truly can be. After all, how long can this good thing last, right? If you reach your goal weight, you'll have to maintain it, so rather fall short and disappoint only yourself!

It's now time to put this in your pipe and smoke it:

> **Your innate skills and abilities, passions and desires are in you for a reason.**
>
> **WHAT YOU LOVE TO DO IS A GOOD INDICATOR OF WHAT YOU SHOULD BE DOING!**

So I ask you, what concepts and ideas stir up your passion? With which ideas could you fall—or have you already fallen—in love?

- Is it creating an excellent home life and helping others do the same?
- Are you in love with the ocean and all that it encompasses?
- Perhaps design (interior/fashion/engineering/architecture) is what energizes you most.
- Or maybe helping young people get properly educated is what accesses your talents, strengths, and contentment levels best.

Some people love writing; others love speaking and motivating. Some cannot get enough of their sport of choice.

Our Interests Point to Our Purpose

Perhaps you *don't* know what you love. Perhaps you have never scratched around on your Life Boat to properly discover your passions.

No one is born *without* dreams, passions, or a love for something. So, don't fear; they are in you somewhere!

The following activity might help you to start dusting them off.

Find yourself a quiet space and take an honest moment.

- *Why* have you not been living your dreams or following your passions?

____

____

____

____

____

____

- What current life frustrations are you experiencing? Why do you think this is so?

- What have you done so far to alleviate these frustrations?

- Have you implemented any **Life Attack** game plans of your own? Have they been successful?

- Which activities or contexts get you rubbing your hands together with excitement and energize you so much that you struggle to leave or stop doing them?

- What did you love to do as a kid? As a teenager? (You were born with your purpose "wired" into you, so you would more than likely have been acting it out from a young age.)

____

____

____

____

____

____

- What gifts and talents have other people affirmed in you?

____

____

____

____

____

- Are you getting an idea of what your talents/longings/ passions might be?

____

____

____

____

____

____

As you read through what you have written, can you feel some longings rising inside you? Are your creative juices starting to flow? Is your mind beginning to slip free from boredom's noose? Are you ready to about-turn and face life head-on?

"So, what am I meant to be doing with my life?" This is something you might have asked for some time now.

Complete the following sentence:

I love ____

What you love **is your purpose. It is as simple as that!**

Having a Life Attack is not as much about finding "the thing" to do with your energy or time as it is finding the *passion* for life that will feed everything you end up doing.

A Quick Aside: The Issue of Talent

> Passion for your purpose is key. But talent or ability comes in a close second.

Just because I'm passionate about singing and love to sing does not mean that I am good enough at it to necessarily become the next *Idols* sensation.

It may, however, mean that I might get to sing and play guitar every day at a luxurious seaside resort for holiday makers—if this is my passion and purpose!

There are, of course, those unfortunate few who insist on doing something they love to do when they really are not gifted in that department. (Do any faces spring to mind?) This is where it helps to have a group of friends who know, love, and care enough about you to find a position for you singing in the 2 a.m. to 4 a.m. slot in a pub that closes at midnight!

LIFE ATTACK TOOL #2: VISION

> **Always Begin with the END in Mind!**

If I asked you where exactly you would like to be in a year's time, would you have an answer for me? What about in five years' time? Ten? Have you ever stopped to *visualize* the future that you would like to have and to be living in clear, crisp detail?

> **If you don't know why you exist and where you are going in life, it is very easy to stagnate.**

On the other hand, if you have a vision for your future—a clear destination in mind of where your Life Boat is going and why it is going there—you will have a reason to get out of bed in the morning and to *make things happen!*

Vision Creates Purpose

Austrian psychiatrist and Holocaust survivor Viktor E Frankl noted during his years in the Second World War death camps that when prisoners believed that their lives had some form of meaning and potential (caring for others and helping others survive, for example), despite the horrors of their circumstances, they were able to *survive* courageously and with dignity.[6]

On the other hand, those who found no meaning to help them rise above their circumstances lived like animals (only concerned with survival and meeting their need for food, rest, etc.) and were less likely to stay alive.

> **The human spirit is resilient if it has a reason to go on.**

This is why I believe that it is vital for you to discover your "why" and to get a clear vision for it.

---

6 Meyer, Werner. Moore, Core. Viljoen, Henning,. 2003. *Personology.* Heinemann Publishers (Pty) Ltd, Cape Town. p. 442.

Using Your Imagination

You might be out of practice with using your imagination positively and creatively. As adults, we tend to pack away the crayons and the toys and shut our imaginations down once we reach a certain age.

We become realistic. Life circumstances teach us to have small expectations. *Failure* drives the nail home on the lid of our dreaming and longing.

In any event, it would look silly for a grown man to run around making noises with a toy airplane, wouldn't it? Or for an adult woman to pretend that she was on a cooking channel while preparing the family dinner.

The truth is, we are all creators! Whether we are aware of it or not, our subconscious thoughts, processes, and memories are alive and active in our day, creating our current realities.

> **"Imagination is more important than knowledge," says Albert Einstein.**

Psychologist Reneau Z. Peurifoy explains that we are constantly evaluating our surroundings with quicker-than-lightning thought processes.[7]

We carry our experiences around in the form of memories and project them onto the next event, often without even realizing it! We use our subconscious imagination to project ourselves into circumstances and to play out the results—often before we even get there.

Much of the time, we use our imaginations for self-defeating purposes.

Ladies, how many times have you dressed for an event with the *potential* reaction of others playing through your head like a movie reel?

7 Peurifoy, Reneau. Z., 2005. *Anxiety, Phobias and Panic: A Step by Step Programme for Regaining Control of Your Life.* Piatkus, London. pp. 7, 85–87.

You try on outfit after outfit, because more often than not, you imagine a negative reaction to your style of choice. And this is probably because you have already had the experience of arriving at some occasion feeling underdressed, overweight, too skinny, dowdy, unappealing or "out."

For men, the pending interview for that job or promotion can often result in an inner war of self-defeating criticism and doubt about one's ability or worthiness.

You become so incapacitated by critical thinking that you never even get around to *applying* for the position.

It is time to harness the "power" of your imagination and actively use it for your own good!

Getting You Started: Imagery Test

Imagine that you have won a holiday to an exotic destination of your choice.

You stand in the departures lounge of the airport, ticket in hand, with butterflies fluttering around excitedly in your stomach.

After kissing envious loved ones left behind, you exit the building and climb up the metal stairs leading into the aeroplane, smiling happily at the neatly turned-out air hostess, who points you to your seat in *first class!*

Your chair is roomy and comfortable. Within minutes of taking your seat, you are handed a tall glass of bubbling champagne and a newspaper. Calming music plays over the speakers. There are gadgets galore for you to acquaint yourself with. As the hours glide by, the sun begins to slowly sink over the horizon, and the breathtaking display of pinks, oranges, and yellows outside your window fades into a black, star-studded night.

When you wake, your aeroplane is within minutes of landing. The view below you of crystal-clear water and a dazzling white shoreline is spellbinding. The aeroplane angles its way down towards the small runway, and you take in the green of jungle and colorful splashes of gaily painted houses.

Life on the island luxuriously stretches out in front of you. Now imagine it for yourself!

Smell the salty sea air. What does the sand underneath your feet feel like on your long beach walks? What island beat envelops you at night as you wine and dine under the stars? Taste the food. See the colors. Smell the smells.

This is the great thing about your imagination. It can transport you to other worlds, free of charge!

It can alter your mood and rouse your sleepy longings and passions.

Hopefully, after the little exercise above, your imagination is humming. Let's not stop there. Let's use it to paint a grand picture of your future.

Writing Down Your Vision

> **You have the ability to build big, beautiful dreams!**

Chew on this statement for a bit. Your inner judge is probably sniffing its nose and telling you otherwise. But it is all true!

From the hot-air balloon to social media, entrepreneurial ventures such as Facebook and Twitter, everything started as a concept in someone's daring imagination and was then dreamed into life.

> **Remember that every *thing* was first a *thought* in someone's mind.**

So why, I ask you, is it such an *impossible* notion that you could make something happen with your dreams?

Remember: You Are the Star in Your Own Movie!

I would now like you to imagine yourself at a celebration. The event being held is for *you* as you enjoy the company of those who have helped you make your dream happen.

Where are you? Who is with you? What does the room look like? What delicious food is being served? What are you drinking? What outfit have you chosen for the special occasion? What have you accomplished? How do you feel about having done this?

Imagine this all in great detail. Use all your senses and the full range of emotions that go with using your imagination.

Why? Because that toothy cannibal of self-doubt needs to be challenged by some positive dreaming and because once you have "tasted" the outcome, you will want it!

Remember: your vision is your own story.

In your story, *you* get to be the leading man or woman, not the "extra" hanging apologetically around in the background.

It is time to write your script, direct it, and star in it. Or, as Mother Teresa so succinctly put it, to "be a pencil in the hand of a writing God."[8]

It is time to start writing a new chapter of your life.

8 http://www.goodreads.com/author/quotes.

Your Vision Statement

You need to define your dream before you can pursue it. You should not head off to Jamaica if you do not know that Jamaica is where you *want* to be heading!

It is time to write down your vision statement.

What would you like to accomplish with your life?

____

____

____

____

____

____

What changes would you like to see happen?

____

____

____

____

____

____

Which of your gifts and talents would you like to see put to work for you?

____

____

____

____

____

____

Don't dream too small! Motivational speaker Les Brown often encourages his audiences to "shoot for the moon." He points out that, should you miss it, you will still find yourself among the stars.

It is important to write your vision statement down in the present tense—as if you are already living it!

Take a look at an example of one of my vision statements. Note that much of what I have included in the statements below *has not happened for me yet.* It is my dream written down in present tense.

> **It's 15 December 2012 and my wife, Michele, and I are so grateful to be visiting one of the many orphanages that have benefited from our "Touching Little Lives One Day at a Time" campaign.**
>
> **We decided to sow 10 percent of all revenue generated through the sale of my book toward supporting orphans with nutritional supplements through Manna Relief.**
>
> **We see the smiles and hear the laughs of these little children and know that we have positively impacted dozens, hundreds, and maybe even thousands of little lives. It is the most heartwarming experience.**
>
> **Michele and I will fly out from here to join our two children for a Christmas skiing holiday in the Alps before I leave for the USA, where I've been invited to speak to a church group on "Having a Life Attack."**

A simpler version of a vision statement could read as follows (again, one of mine):

> **I am living my purpose and excited to be working on my second book, which is to be released in March 2012.**

Now it is your turn. Simply dream and then write the dream down as if you are slap-bang in the middle of it, in as much detail as you desire.

At this point, do not ask *how* regarding this vision. A 70 percent *why* (a strong and gripping vision) will beat a 30 percent *how* in a boxing ring any day!

Give strength to your vision by claiming it as a possibility. You need to give it a fighting chance to get off the ground, so don't load *hows* into your shotgun just yet.

Dream about it as much as possible and as often as possible!

Write down your vision:

Is your vision as gripping to you as a good rugby match or a whodunit movie?

Does it make all things good and exciting rise up in you?

Are you virtually salivating at the concept of putting it into play? Are your fingers twitching? Is your foot tapping? Do you need a moment to wonder at your daring?

> **A life vision that captivates all your energy, excitement and attention is one that you will have the tenacity to follow, no matter what might be thrown your way to prevent it.**

LIFE ATTACK TOOL #3: GOALS

You cannot sit on a couch the whole day long, envisioning yourself owning a gleaming, red Ferrari.

Trust me, as creatively as you might be able to imagine one purring up your driveway, the bottom line is that vision without *action* is useless.

Your vision needs an action plan. It is as simple as that.

If your vision is the direction in which your Life Boat is headed (Jamaica), then your goals are the coordinates or pathway you will use to get there.

> **The purpose of a goal is to benchmark your progress.**

Setting specific, realistic, and measurable goals breaks your vision down into specific, realistic, and measurable steps.[9]

Setting and *achieving* small goals along the way will also help you gain confidence. The bigger destination up ahead seems feasible when you can tick or cross little boxes next to smaller victories:

Repair Boat ☑

Stock Cabin ☑

Get your arse off this island! ☑

Setting goals:

When setting goals, remember to:

1. Start where you are. Be realistic.

   You need to start setting goals from where you actually find yourself in life—financially, relationally, and emotionally. The raw material that you have for your Life Attack Challenge is *you!*

---

9 Maxwell, John. C., 2009. *Put Your Dreams to the Test: 10 Questions to Help You See It and Seize It.* Thomas Nelson. Nashville, Tennessee, p. 102.

Start with what you do have—degrees, skills, experience, talents, contacts, resources—and then work your way out from there.

For example, perhaps you would like to sail around the world carrying medical supplies to third world countries.

You might have a medical degree, some experience in sailing, but no benevolent, rich uncle waiting in the wings to throw vast amounts of money at you.

To accomplish this dream, you may need sponsors or another means to raise funds, some more instruction in sailing, perhaps some more languages under your belt, a team to share your vision, a yacht, etc.

Can you already start to see what goals might need to be set in order for this dream to become a reality?

2. Be specific.

A specific destination will require specific goals to get you there.

It is true that life is not half as predictable as we would like it to be. Achieving your goals will never be an exact science—things are likely to crop up that will alter your route a bit here and there.

This is okay. Keep your destination (the vision) in clear focus, but enjoy the ride it takes you on. Be flexible.

All of this aside, it is still important to set *specific* goals. Your list of goals is not a list of wishful thinking.

Vague goals point to a vague harbor in a vague port on a vague island somewhere.

Vagueness is not nearly as motivating as a definite plan.

A vague goal such as, "I want to get fit" can be whipped into shape by rewording it:

"It is 28 February 2011, and I am so thankful that I am walking five kilometers per day at a brisk pace. I have lost three centimeters around my waist, and I don't feel like a ten-ton elephant has sat on my chest—I can breathe! Yippee!"

Remember, there is nothing wrong with setting time limits to your goals. In this way, your goal achievement becomes *measurable.*

Have you started walking five kilometers a day by February? No? Then you need to either rework that goal or work harder towards achieving it.

Put Your Goals to Work

There is a vast difference between *setting* a goal and actually *achieving* it.

While writing down and clarifying your goals are a vital part of living into your purpose, putting those goals into action is of even more import.

Goal-setting and achieving comes through practice. This is why, while having your Life Attack, I would strongly encourage you to go about setting yourself small, achievable Life Attack Goals on a daily basis.

> **These daily goals will come from your long-term goals.**

For example, if your vision is to become a helicopter pilot in the Democratic Republic of Congo, and one of your long-term goals is to attend a flight school to make this dream a reality, then a daily goal could be to take some books out of the library to read up on your favorite topic or to visit a bank to talk to them about a student loan.

A daily goal for an artist could be to finish a certain section of a painting by the end of the day or to visit another artist friend for some coffee and inspiration.

The bottom line is that it is both vital and recommended that you work *daily* towards achieving your dream!

Goal Cards

I carry around on my person small pieces of cardboard, which I call Goal Cards. On these get written my Daily Life Attack Goals.

They go where I go, so I can keep them in front of my easily distracted nose.

I pull them out whenever I need a reminder as to what I want to accomplish in my day. They keep me focused. They help me to maximize the time I have in my day.

As I cross my achieved goals off the list, these small wins help me to create a *template of success* in my mind. I become a goal-achieving person.

Visualization Board

Many of us are *visually* stimulated people. What we see inspires and motivates us. This is why I would also recommend that you create for yourself a Visualization Board on which you can physically build and represent your dreams.

Use pictures out of magazines, phrases out of a newspaper clipping, quotes, doodles, personal encouragements, fabric, paint, objects from nature (you name it) in order to create for yourself a vibrant, visual reminder of where you are heading.

You can build this board in a day or gradually as you go.

Your Visualization Board is your love letter to your dream, so enjoy it!

The Visualization Board could also be an effective tool for you to use if you are still struggling with the "what" and "why" question of your purpose.

As you paste, sew, or hammer objects, images, and concepts onto your board that are appealing to you, look for a common thread. The creative process is a very revealing one. You might just find your purpose staring back at you.

Remember, while creating your Visualization Board:

- Hang it where you can see it. It is there to inspire you! You want it to trigger your creativity and help you feed your dream.
- Don't be critical or perfectionistic about it. In the words of Nike, "just do it!"
- Don't let others be critical about it—it's *your* dream. But at the same time, when you feel comfortable, ask for feedback. Your friends and family might be curious as to what you are getting up to, and they might be able to give you some positive pointers to dwell on as your vision visually unfolds.

LIFE ATTACK TOOL #4: ACTION!

You have a vision. You have some short-term goals to fulfill this long-term vision. Now get moving and get out there!

> **A dream unfolds on the trot, as you get your body, mind, and resources moving in its direction.**

You might not yet feel that you have *all* you need to get your dream ball rolling, but remember, a Life Attack is a *process,* and anything that you do towards fulfilling your dream is progress.

So, start today by …

1. Feeding your dream

If you love writing, frequent book shops (secondhand and new), or your local library; follow authors online via Twitter or Facebook; join a book club; sit for ages in coffee shops and in public spaces, people-watching and absorbing every detail.

Start a blog. Interview people on subject matters that interest you. Get those creative juices flowing.

If finances, or the lack of qualifications or "street cred" are standing in the way, then become a volunteer. Work your way up the ladder. Serve tea, do odd jobs, eat some humble pie.

Many a success story has come from someone willing to put in the hard work.

Be daring! Would it be helpful for you to get in touch with that famous disc jockey for coffee to pick her brain about how she climbed her vocational ladder? *Do it!*

If nothing comes of it, choose someone else who might be more willing or available to share what they know with you.

Don't see failure as failure, because it isn't!

Mistakes are lessons in disguise. Did trying stretch you? Did it make you grow? Have you learned something positive? Did it feed your passion for more?

Don't dwell on negative experiences you might have on this journey. Take what you can learn from them, say thank you, and then move on!

2. "Skilling up" where need be

It is never too late to study or "skill up" in your specific area of talent or gifting.

I love the real-life example that we have in the highly gifted South African artist and "boykie," Duncan Stewart.[10]

After studying graphic design at the Natal Technikon, and working in the industry in Johannesburg for seven years, Duncan decided that it was time for change.

Although already in his late twenties (most commonly regarded as an age for "responsible settling down"), Duncan planned to do the exact opposite: he turned his attention towards furthering his studies at the Lorenzo de Medici Institute—an art school in Italy.

By uprooting himself and relocating to foreign soil, Duncan aimed to do two things: firstly, to grow his faith and dependency levels on God *significantly*. (What better way to do this than to move to a foreign country, to live in a foreign culture, where he would be less capable of fending for himself?) Secondly, to raise his technical and professional game:

> When you play with a better tennis player, you lift your game. When walking the streets that Masters like Dante, Da Vinci, Galileo, Michelangelo walked, something gets transferred. Call it romance, call it dreaming or aspirations … but one begins to see oneself in a brighter light.

Duncan raised money for his adventure by rallying sponsorship for each kilometer that he rode on a cycle trip from Johannesburg to Cape Town—a distance of some 1,400 kilometers!

---

10 See Duncan's inspiring artwork on *www.duncanstewart.co.za.*

He sold most of his possessions—from his car to his clothes—and cashed in all his policies.

He also organized black-tie events where he auctioned off his artwork.

He was a man with a vision in mind and a plan to make it happen.

Armed with some cash, his trusty mountain bike, and his paint box (his luggage only arrived three days after he did), Duncan found himself in Italy, in need of a place to stay.

> My rent was far more than I had budgeted for, so I had great need to trust God for my accommodation. I prayed about a spot in the country and God moved mountains to find me a place to stay. I ended up renting a room in a 16th Century barn that had been restored. The barn was located in an orchard above a quaint village called Fornello. A car was even thrown in as part of the rental agreement …

Duncan's inspiring story does not end there. He shares that he had always imagined himself marrying a princess.

During the course of his studies, he met a young woman by the name of Marie-Natalie Elizabeth Margaretha Paula von Heyden-Linden in the Restoration Laboratory at the Lorenzo de Medici Institute.

Duncan and Natalie were soon mutually smitten, but Duncan still had to do some serious persuading to win her family's trust and get them to agree to their courtship. She was, after all, from a long line of German nobility.

The story ends with the two wed in the charming little village of Cabrieres in the South of France.

Duncan is just a person—like any other person. What sets him apart is his inspirational willingness and daring to grow and invest in his artistic talent and be stretched beyond his comfort zones.

Go on and be inspired by him to do likewise!

LIFE ATTACK TOOL #5: THOUGHT LIFE

Have you ever heard of the concept of learned helplessness?

It's a term that psychologists have coined to describe the state in which we find ourselves when negative upbringings, contexts, and life experiences have inclined our perceptions and thought processes towards hopelessness and negativity.

Learned helplessness is the "I Cannot Because ..." syndrome. It is essentially *learned stuck-ness*.

Perhaps your Life Boat has been heading off in the wrong direction for so long that you have resigned yourself to never getting to where you want to be.

Instead, you float wherever the tides take you, and you may have even forgotten how to paddle!

If people ask you why you don't about turn and choose your own life destination, you point to controlling parents, a long list of negative comments received over the years, a childhood of poverty (with no spare cash for you to pursue your interests), your failed attempts at following a specific course, and the like.

Maybe your Life Boat has taken such a bashing from life's storms, or knocks from other people in their Life Boats, that you have learned to *accommodate* the water swirling around your ankles, the way your boat tilts dangerously to one side, and the general sad look of disrepair around you.

You now just sit staring bleakly at the horizon, waiting for the next storm to hit or the next reckless paddler to bump on by.

All of this is no good!

Thoughts Become Things

One of the *key* ingredients to any Life Attack is to create a healthy and positive thought life.

Our perspectives and attitudes can make or break us.

According to the writer of Proverbs, "as a man thinketh, so is he."[11]

James Allen, author of *As a Man Thinketh,* agrees with this sentiment: "You are today where your thoughts have brought you; you will be tomorrow where your thoughts take you."[12]

The thoughts that we dwell on turn into the words we speak, which then report to our actions. Our actions lead to habits, which become tenacious companions on our journeys and prevent us doing differently.

Whose Voice Is it Anyway?

"I don't have enough people skills to pull my dream off."

"I'm too ugly to be loved."

"I'm stupid."

"I'll never be good enough."

Often, when we have self-defeating thoughts that cycle through our heads, instead of catching them, scrutinizing each one closely for its accuracy, and then speaking back some "now you listen here ..." truth, we roll over with our feet in the air and twitch in various stages of defeat.

May I suggest that it is far more helpful to become *objective* about your thought life.

By objective, I mean that there is no reason why you should own every thought that comes into your head just because it is *in* your head.

---

11 Proverbs 23:7.
12 http://www.goodreads.com/quotes.

Much of what we consciously and subconsciously think about ourselves stems from past life experiences.

Our earliest experiences can often be the most defining. Whether good or bad, they leave deposits in our judgment that shape our thinking and speaking.

For example, a child whose father told him from the age of four that he would amount to nothing does not have the mental ability to agree or disagree with that parent. The father's voice becomes the child's voice in a self-defeating cycle.

Many years on, that child does not even know how to differentiate between the two voices. He just hears one voice—his own! It *sounds* like him, and it's been saying the same things for years. Therefore, it *must* be true.

Not so!

The Five Whys[13]

Can you see why is very important that you get to the bottom of your thinking?

The next time you have a particularly debilitating thought, sit yourself down and ask yourself five "whys."

By hounding a particular thought with a why question, you will not only be able to develop the valuable skill of "taking every thought captive,"[14] but you will also soon discover that *many* of your thoughts are layered.

What you see at the surface is not necessarily what is hidden at the centre.

Below is an example of the "five whys" exercise:

---

13 Bates, Valerie & Yarnell, Mark. 2009. The Lotus Code Accelerator. Networking Times Press. USA. p52
14 2 Corinthians 10:5

Self-Defeating Thought: I am not a people's person.

Why? I don't feel comfortable around people.

Why? I am worried about what they will think of me.

Why? I have had some bad experiences previously.

Why? I was misunderstood.

Why? We were young, and my friends did not then have the capacity to understand me.

By the end of the five whys, you should have more answers!

Hopefully, you will be able to put your fears into context. You will be able to find their roots and begin to address them accordingly.

For example, the conclusion given above that "We were young, and my friends did not then have the capacity to understand me" can be reformulated as some positive self-talk:

"Previously, *I was misunderstood—but that is because we were young. One group of children in my childhood not being able to relate to me does not mean that no one will be able to relate to me. I need to make better conclusions for my life now that I am no longer a child. I chose to hide then, but now need to let people know me …"*

Cultivating truthful and positive thoughts and words about ourselves is the hardest part of all!

Bates and Yarnell liken it to pushing a large boulder up and over a hill.[15] Here, all the sweating and heaving happens at the bottom of the hill and continues right up to the top. Once that boulder reaches the top, however, it is free sailing (or rolling) from there.

Consider your words and thoughts to be the boulder.

Your learning to become objective about your thoughts is the hard slog up the hill. Eventually, however, the hard slog evens out, as positive thinking and speaking become a habit.

15 The Lotus Code Accelerator. Networking Times Press. USA. p 52

You grow so accustomed to catching your negative thoughts and preventing them from sabotaging you that you soon feel as if you are trotting on *down* the hill, with your thought life rolling along easily in front of you.

You know the quip "I need that, like, yesterday"? Well, you need to practice positive thinking "like, yesterday!" So go on and do it!

Prosperity Consciousness

I recently interviewed Paul Martinelli to glean his insights on how change in his own thinking has altered the course of his life.

Paul journeyed from being a stuttering high school dropout, hailing from a working-class family, to becoming a business leader and entrepreneur. He is also an acclaimed international speaker, teacher and coach[16].

He shared with me that, as a young man, he did not realise that he *could* change the direction and results of his life. He believed that life had dealt him a number of cards and he was stuck playing them. It never even occurred to him that he could throw these back into the centre of the table and ask for a new hand, or that he could be his own dealer.

Once he began to understand the control he did have over his own life and the need to change his perceptions about his life's potential, he was able to make many positive life changes.

> "Many of us think that we do not control our thinking, but we do! You hear people often say, 'It's not my fault I think this way', but this is not true. If we don't like our eyebrows, we tweeze them and if we don't like our noses, we go for surgery and have a nose job. We take control. Similarly, many of us need "thinking jobs"; we need to reconstruct our thinking."

He pointed out that an intellectual understanding alone of the power of one's daily thoughts is not adequate enough for us to see positive change in our lives, nor is running a positive mantra through our heads as we

16 http://www.paulmartinelli.net/about/index.html

go about our daily lives, believing that we just have to trick fate by a positive confession to become successful people

Rather, he believes that we need to *personalise* the truth that our lives can change for the better. We need to truly believe it.

> "Everyone can be an Abundance Thinker. We can step out under a night sky and see thousands of stars above our heads, or onto millions of grains of sand at the oceans edge and we can recognise that God expresses abundantly and that there is enough of everything. The key is to develop a Prosperity Consciousness instead. There is a subtle difference between the two.
>
> An Abundance Thinker thinks, 'there is enough', while a person with a Prosperity Consciousness follows with, '...and it is *for me*.' "

Paul went on to share that the big change happened for him when he realised that there was enough (of life, resources and possibility etc.) for him, not only for the guy 'next door'.

He realised that he was in control of his life, the flipside of this being that then he was also responsible for what happened in his life.

"We often ask ourselves, '*Who* is the matter with me?!' We blame everyone else for our circumstances – from our bankers, employees and clients, to family members and significant others.

> I heard someone once say that if another person can make you mad, sad or glad, then you have been had! The fact that I *can* think what I want to think about myself, my life and my future makes me responsible for that future, which means that I need to stop blame shifting. Blame shifting prevents me from taking responsibility and control."

Spiritual Slipstream

Many people find themselves bogged down in life. They feel trapped in their circumstances. It does not help them to watch others freely float on by with smiles on their faces while they find themselves battling the mire of their circumstances.

I asked Paul how such people could get *unstuck*. What steps could they take to slipstream beyond their current restrictions?

> "Firstly, we need to differentiate between those people who are conditionally stuck and those who are just in a funk of depression.
>
> My following recommendation is not for those people who are battling mental challenges like chronic depression (I would encourage them to seek the professional help they would need to cope with such realities) but for those who are physically and mentally healthy but stuck nonetheless.
>
> I have come to realise that if you are healthy and stuck then you are unhealthy *spiritually*.
>
> Our journey out of restriction is not a horizontal journey, but a vertical one - about 18 inches from our head to our hearts. We need to look at our spiritual selves and contemplate where we are on our spiritual journeys.
>
> By this I mean that we need to recognise that we have a connection to the universe and that we matter enough to be connected to the "Source". An understanding of this will help us live into our full potential.
>
> Many of us look intently at the conditions and circumstances of our contexts to find a solution to get us out. But there are no ropes or ladders in a quicksand pit. You are never going to find yourself free of the quicksand by looking

deeply in it for solutions; you need to look *beyond* it for the answers."

Paul believes that as we shift our awareness to understand that we are part of a bigger picture, we can begin to realise that it is OK to fail, to experience fear and to take risks in our lives nevertheless. A change in awareness, through spiritual contemplation, helps us begin to move out of our stuck places.

Questions like 'Why does this keep happening to me?' and 'Who is the matter with me?' can take a backseat in our lives; we no longer need to run like hamsters on the wheel of our circumstances, feeling incapable of jumping off!

Setting Your Intention

Einstein once said that the significant problems we encounter cannot be solved at the same level of thinking we were at when we created them[17]. Thoughts that made you fat, for example, will not help you lose weight; thoughts that have resulted in broken relationships will not help you experience healthier, harmonious ones.

One thing that has become abundantly clear to me on my own journey as a speaker, coach and now author is the need to wake up each day and set my intention for the day.

I do this by first visualizing how I want my day to progress. This includes who I want to meet that day, how I will both be a blessing and receive blessings wherever I go and how favour will follow me every minute of my day.

Each morning I have a picture in my mind of the type of person that I called to be and I ask myself in moments of prayer and meditation how that person might speak or act, walk and talk, eat and exercise.

This practice has greatly changed the results and direction of my life and it will do the same for you too!

17 http://www.soularenergy.net/Spirituality_Metaphysical_Quotes.html

Firefighters versus Firelighters

The honest truth is that the company we keep greatly influences our outlook on life. "Birds of a feather flock together" and "misery loves company" are two aptly coined phrases.

It is important, in your Life Attack journey, to actively seek out positive, encouraging companions for the road.

I have heard such people being referred to as "firelighters."

Firelighters are positive individuals. They believe in their own dreams and are ready to believe in yours. They are honest and will give you the constructive criticism you need, but they won't grab a shotgun and proceed to displace you from the sky with it!

Fire*fighters,* on the other hand, will douse your small flame of enthusiasm with criticism and negativity any chance they can get.

Les Brown says that some people are so negative that when they walk into a dark room, they begin to develop. Avoid them!

Although it is virtually impossible to be around firelighters at all times, you should try to get healthy doses of them.

Bottom line—be mindful of the company you keep.

It might be beneficial to spend less time with that friend who wants to pull you down into the mire of negativity and more time with those who will build you up.

Give positive thinking a fighting chance!

The "Ja-But" Challenge

Your thoughts mixed with your emotions ultimately lead to the actions your take and your resultant behavior.

As I mentioned previously, much of our self-talk leans towards negativity.

Every grand, intuitive idea that you've had is very often counteracted by an immediate negative thought from your Inner Judge, who says something like, "Yes, but … I can't do that because …" Your Inner Judge then goes on to list every reason under the sun, and you listen attentively!

It's time to make a shift in your thinking. Enter … drumroll, please … the "JA-BUT"[18] Challenge!

Similar to Mark Victor Hansen and Robert G. Allan's 'Yes, But' Challenge[19](from *The One Minute Millionare: The Enlightened Way to Wealth),* the Sean Willard "JA-BUT"' challenge is designed to help you practically tackle your patterns of critical thinking.

For the JA-BUT challenge, you will need a JA-BUT elastic wristband. This you will wear 24/7. Every time you catch yourself thinking a negative thought or expressing a negative, limiting belief or excuse about anyone or anything, you then *snap* your JA-BUT wristband against your wrist. Or you invite others to do it for you.

Yes, it hurts!

Wearing this wristband 24/7 and snapping it each time you think a negative or self-defeating thought will quickly change your thinking, your speaking, and ultimately, the results you get in your life!

You will be shocked to discover how many negative thoughts whizz through your brain every day. You will also quickly learn that you can *choose* the thoughts you want to dwell on and cultivate.

You can start actively learning to accept the good ones and to replace the negative ones and—voila!—begin to feel good and live well.

Once the red welt is no longer visible (okay, now I sound like a sadist), you can invert the wristband so that your positive affirmation reads: "Yes, I can!"

---

18 For non South African readers, "JA" is the Afrikaans word for *yes.* Here the J is pronounced as if it is the Y in *yellow* or *yes.* The A is pronounced as if it is the A in *art:* YA. That's right!

19

You might also choose to snap yourself every time you hang around negative people making negative comments to remind you to:

1. Change the subject;
2. Say something positive about the person or situation;
3. Walk away from that negative conversation;
4. Keep quiet and don't participate; or
5. Clearly state that you no longer want to gossip or speak negatively and excuse yourself if they want to continue.

LIFE ATTACK TOOL #6: LIFE COACH

We humans can be rather lazy by nature. We know we should exercise, but we don't; we know we should budget, but we don't; we know we should plan ahead, but we don't; we know that we should eat more healthily and avoid those fast-food drive-thrus—but we don't! Bone idleness runs stubbornly through our veins.

Many people have found that it is quite helpful to partner up with someone who will motivate and encourage them to keep on going in their life endeavors.

Jogs around the neighborhood and implementing a healthy eating plan are so much easier if there is someone else to suffer along with you!

That is why the last tool in your Life Attack Challenge will be to find yourself a life coach to keep you motivated on your Life Attack Journey.

I liken a life coach to a gym coach. Within your first few visits to the gym, you were probably weighed and had a fitness program helpfully worked out for you. Do you follow it? Probably not!

Left to your own devices at the gym, you will more than likely avoid the most challenging of exercise equipment and make a beeline for "all things manageable."

Enter gym coach, an enthusiastic individual with a six-pack you can only dream about, who will push you beyond your capabilities to become the mean, sleek muscle machine he or she knows you can be.

Gym coach will not let you do twenty pushups instead of thirty. Gym coach will hold your weight and fitness goals in front of your sweating head as you run another so many kilometers on the treadmill.

And, although you might happily kill gym coach on occasion, all the encouragement and affirmation heaped on you as you push through each gym session, and come out on the other end feeling healthy and fit, means that you ultimately *love* and appreciate gym coach *a great deal!*

Your *life* coach might not come with a "ripped" six-pack, but whoever you choose needs to inspire as much of a love-hate relationship within you as a gym coach might.

Your life coach will need to keep you accountable and encouraged along your Life Attack journey, so he or she will need to be familiar with your vision and goals and be good at helping you keep on track.

THE LIFE ATTACK CHALLENGE:

Lessons learned along the way.

"Cherish your visions; cherish your ideals; cherish the music that stirs in your heart, the beauty that forms in your mind, the loveliness that drapes your purest thoughts, and if you but remain true to them, your world will at last be built."

— James Allen

Selling my business was a huge relief. Initially, I felt quite disgruntled at having spent twenty years of my life not living according to my dreams. Now I can see that those twenty years served as a foundation phase for who I am and where I currently am in life and that it was imperative that I went through those years of experience.

You might currently be sitting on an island reef far, far away from your purpose, staring bleakly at the horizon, contemplating the years lost, chewing on a coconut and wishing it were not so.

I would encourage you to take a few minutes and to make a list of what you have possibly gained and learned, irrespective of your rudderless state.

What skills have you picked up? What have you learned about yourself these past years? These are all going with you on your new journey of life purpose discovery—and it's useful to know what is in your backpack!

I often share with people the analogy of life as the Great Hiking Adventure.

From this analogy, I teach a few important things. On this hiking adventure, it is vital to:

1. Drop the Bulley Beef

If you open up your backpack and find blame, unforgiveness, and resentment inside, then you have a backpack full of Bulley Beef.[20]

If you know anything about hiking, then you will know that this is a dumb idea. There is nothing fun about lugging heavy tins around with you up a mountain pass or over rocks and across rivers! Try it sometime if you don't believe me.

> **It is important that you travel light on your Life Attack journey. Don't play the blame game. *Drop* the Bulley Beef!**

Hard things might have happened to and around you over which you have had no control. It is easy to begin to point fingers and to blame your current life situation on others. *Don't!* It is not going to get you anywhere.

It is important to be honest about any hurt, disappointment, and anger you are feeling. But hanging on to Bulley Beef will keep you in a victim mode.

"Harboring unforgiveness is like drinking poison and then waiting for someone else to die![21]" This well-known adage highlights a sobering reality that emotional pain and resentment, left to fester, can be more psychologically detrimental for us in the long run than counting our losses and moving on.

The better option, therefore, is to start to take responsibility for your own life. Start pushing forward. Start forgiving and letting go. Unpack your backpack and get rid of that unnecessary luggage.

---

20 Corned beef/tinned meat.

21 Author unknown

2. **Enjoy the Journey**

On a hike, I am one of those people who is so fixated on getting to the halfway hut that scenery, vegetation, waterfalls, conversation, and wildlife along the way passes in a blur.

I am often so destination-focused that I forget to enjoy the ride!

> **It is important to learn how to live in the *moment*. On your Life Attack journey, be sure to enjoy the process—*all* of it!**

Achieving your goals and life vision is a waste of time if you don't enjoy the route you take in getting there or the people who join you on the journey!

If it is helpful, start a daily journal to document your travels. Include aspects for which you are grateful, things you have learned, and minor victories along the way. Stop to smell the wildflowers! Take little detours. Absorb the entire experience.

3. **Appreciate the view at the top!**

I have to confess that I often fear *success* more than I do failure.

I liken it to climbing to the top of a mountain, planting my flag, and then quickly heading back down to base camp without looking at the view or taking the time to savor my achievement.

Why would I do that? Perhaps I am worried that after all that hard slog, the view will be disappointing. Perhaps I am worried that all I will see ahead are more mountains to climb, and this will be disillusioning.

Being great in one moment puts the pressure on one to be great in many more. *Underachievement* is often a far more comfortable reality on which to chew. If I fly under the radar, no one will expect any grand heroics from me.

I have to learn to enjoy the view at the top, pressure-free. Again, it comes down to living in the moment.

Our "nows" often get robbed by our anxieties about what is up ahead. In some instances I need to take undue pressure off myself and in others, I need to step up to the plate.

Summary

I am told that there is no difference between the size of a normal tree's seed and that of a bonsai.

Among other contributors, it is the *size of the pot* it is planted in that plays a large role in curtailing a bonsai's growth.

Many of us are like this diminutive tree. We have planted our potential in restrictive spaces and are not experiencing much growth.

My passion and purpose is to help you bust your "pot" open, in order for you to stretch, grow, and reach your full potential.

I have suggested some Life Attack tools for you to do this:

- Passion
- Vision
- Goals
- Action
- A positive thought life
- A life coach
- A few vital life lessons.

See me standing on the shores of your last port of stay, jumping up and down, waving at you as you launch ahead on your Life Attack journey.

Remember, in all things pertaining to your life, *you have a choice to make about the direction, quality, and flavor of your journey, and only you can make it!*

"… when each day is the same as the next, it's because people fail to recognize the good things that happen in their lives every day the sun rises."

Paulo Coelho, The Alchemist

Introduction

"Love is a creative act and you are built to play the part."
—Tania Ahlfeldt[22]

You are in your Life Boat.

The wind gustily fills your brilliantly white sails with "vooma."[23] You enjoy the newfound feeling of purpose and potential racing through your veins. The dolphins leap happily in your wake, and the sea birds drift above you in lazy circles.

Just then, one of your loved ones appears from the cabin below and asks you to help out with the dishes. The theme song that has been playing in your head winds to an abrupt halt and you snap back edgily, "Not now! Can't you see I'm *busy*?!" Or you might simply choose to ignore them.

Is there anything wrong with this picture?

We humans can get rather preoccupied with ourselves, our gadgets, and our pleasures! We give most of our love and attention to our work, our hobbies, and our passions and then run empty on love reserves for those who matter most to us.

> **The bottom line is that it won't do anybody any good for you to finally live on purpose, moving towards your potential, if you do not live as someone who loves.**

22 http://thecreativemoment.wordpress.com/2010/09/20/feeling-the-love.
23 AKA "power."

By "love," I am not referring to *romantic* love alone. I am talking about "taking-out-the-garbage" love; I am talking about "visiting-granny-over-the-weekend" love; and I am talking about love levels for life in general.

Love Boat or Slave Galley?

You might now have a boat that knows where it's going, but what is its condition?

- Is it a love boat or a castaway boat?
- Is it brightly painted and inviting, or is it a slave galley, with everyone fearfully walking around you as if on eggshells?
- Does your boat, on occasion, get crammed full of people who share life with you and who know that you love them, or do you merely endure your travelling companions and hope that they leave you alone as soon as possible?

I recently invited a bunch of people to take part in a survey to gauge their work, play, and love contentment levels. This survey revealed that a number of people are aware that their closest relationships are in need of loving attention.[24]

When asked whether they were really giving their *all* in their love relationships, many said they were; an equal number confessed to keeping something back in their reserve tanks.

Reasons given for holding back love from their loved ones included fear of rejection, past relational disappointments, financial concerns, the newness of a relationship, an empty love tank, and wariness of giving more than the other person in the relationship.

However, as one wise soul on the survey pointed out:

> **"Giving your all to those who are close to you is the only way to earn the right to hope for something in return."**

24 Dead or Dreaming? Survey on: *http://www.surveymonkey.com.*

In that light, I believe that the next section of this book is as vital to your Life Attack journey as your Life Attack itself.

The Love Attack Challenge is for those who:

- Find themselves merely "existing" in their relationships and who want to change and start *really* loving *full out!*
- Are in need of a wheelbarrow full of sugar for their lemony, unloving countenances.
- Need to recapture the essence of loving people and life in a practical way.
- Know that their love life could do with the challenge!
- Want to live a life of significance.

So, what are we waiting for? One, two, three … let's go!

Our Story

"You never lose by loving. You *always* lose by holding back."
—Barbara De Angelis

I know that bookstores are crowded with books on love in every guise. I am also very aware that I am no Dr. Phil or Dr. Ruth.

This means that I do not have the time, expertise, or desire to deal with every aspect of this colossal subject. But let me tell you what I *do* have going for me in this department which might be of benefit to you:

I am a guy who wants to love *full out!*

> Whether it be my wife, my children, my family or friends, I am past the stage where loving them at 50 percent capacity is regarded as "okay".
>
> I believe that life is a gift and a journey that we are given to appreciate to its fullest every day.
>
> Within this gift package called life, we get to unpack the things we love to do (our purpose); we get to find people we love to be with (building our love lives); and we get to reach outside our immediate circles to people beyond our love lives (to grow our people love).
>
> We also get to adventure on and explore a world we can learn to admire, respect, and appreciate (expanding our planet love).
>
> Life is about loving!

Did you say 100 percent?!

Do you remember wishing, hoping, and "cannot-waiting" for some future date or event because it was going to be much better than the present moment?

When you were in grade five, for example, you couldn't wait for grade eight. Then when you reached grade eight, you couldn't wait for the day you finished high school.

When you were in university, you couldn't wait to graduate, and when you were dating, you couldn't wait for marriage.

I'm sure you get the point.

Whatever happened to living *in the moment* and *loving* that moment?

My question to you is simple: are you giving love your all? Can you say that you are present to life and loving it full-out? If not, why not?

> The love condition of your Life Boat is *your* choice.

If no one wants to join you on your boat or to share ocean space with you; if your boat is a dingy grey from a lack of loving; or if life around you appears dull, cautious, reserved, or uninspiring, then there is only one thing for you to do: *Stop blaming everybody and everything else around you (if you have been doing so) and take 100 percent responsibility for your life!*

The bottom line is that you can continue to pace yourself and give 50, 60, or 70 percent of your best to people, your passions, and to this planet, or you can decide (our key word again) to start loving and living full-out—at an exciting and daring 100 percent.

The next few chapters of this book will deal with how to go about doing this.

But First ... Our Story

My wife, Michele, and I learned how to appreciate this gift of life the hard way.

Our story goes like this: Michele and my Life Boats crossed paths when she was fifteen (just a pip!) and I was eighteen.

The moment I saw her, I remember thinking that *this* was my wife! I even told this to the friend I was talking with at the time. I liked this girl!

As I stood around, chatting to my group of friends and sipping coffee, I found my gaze wandering across the room in her direction. I could not stop admiring how beautiful she was. Even at that age, she had a quiet, inner strength and resolve to which I was drawn.

It wasn't long before I invited her aboard my Life Boat for a chat, and we spoke late into the night, laughing and enjoying our new friendship.

We hung around each other and dated for the next five years, and then, because we agreed on important Life Boat matters and I now loved this girl and she loved me, we decided to make it permanent.

When we finally got married, I was only twenty-three and Michele just twenty.

Having known each other for some time already, Michele and I saw no need to wait very long before beginning to grow our family. We agreed to start trying for our first baby within the first three to four years of our marriage.

When Michele fell pregnant in the spring of 1994, we were ecstatic that our plans to start a family had worked out. We were looking forward to growing our small fleet to three.

Sadly, that December, we lost that first child due to a miscarriage. Although it was a very tough experience, we pressed on, confident that we would soon be parents.

Four years and three more miscarriages later, however, our confidence and hopes were crushed. The pain of the losses had taken their toll on us as individuals.

Michele is a born mother. She is, hands down, the most incredibly patient, loving, and caring individual I have ever met. The fact that she couldn't enjoy loving her own children tore me apart.

I was exceptionally busy in my pharmacy and found this to be a great escape from our pain, but even I was floored by our last loss. *Four* miscarriages, and for no apparent reason.

I will not do Michele's experience of our journey justice if I told it, so here are some of her own thoughts on the matter.

> Those four years were a rollercoaster of emotions for me: from the expectation and pure joy of knowing that there was life inside of me, to the fervent hope that this little life would just *hang in there* and survive.
>
> I wondered and worried on what more I could do or *not do* to keep our babies. Each emotional rollercoaster ride finally ended with me having to face the devastation of yet another loss—and we did not even know why!
>
> I am a qualified teacher, so children are part of who I am, and the desire to have one of my own was *great*. I knew in my heart that Sean and I would have a baby—this I did not doubt—but the road to get there definitely was *not* the one that we had envisioned!
>
> Frustration was a huge emotion for me at the time. Anger too! A good friend decided to fall pregnant over that period, and "bingo" it just happened. "Not fair!" was all I was thinking, while struggling to be truly happy for her.
>
> It was hard to live and love each day when I longed for the time when I would have my baby. I had to make a conscious decision and effort to embrace that period and to *gain* all I could from the experience in order to grow from it.

I believe that all things happen for a reason and that we have to push through and grab as much out of life as we can before we can come out the other side.

Throughout this time, I did feel God's hand on us. The promises that He had made were in our hearts, and I clung to them.

For Sean and me, this was a crucial time of drawing from one another, standing together, and loving the *now*—as hard as it was to do so.

It is bittersweet for me to look back to *then,* when my two children are running around and shouting in my *"now,"* but the love that I embrace today and the hugs that I feel have made the journey worthwhile …

Hope Renewed

In 1998, I met a young patient who shared with me her own story of struggling to have children and of her ultimate victory when she gave birth to a healthy baby.

She had used a progesterone product over the course of her pregnancy, with great success, and Michele and I, deciding that there was nothing for us to lose, chose to follow this young woman's lead.

When Michele fell pregnant in about November of that year, we prayerfully pursued a new course of action that ended with me giving my wife cortisone injections for many months.

How gracious Michele was to me at the time. I was a man on a mission to save my family, even if it meant turning her into a human pin cushion to achieve this!

My first few attempts to give her the injection were pitiful, to say the least. Somehow injecting your own family member seems a lot more challenging than a stranger or a patient.

Finally, in July 1999, Michele gave birth to our son, Nathan. Despite the miscarriage of our fifth child after Nathan was born, Michele was able to fall pregnant and carry our daughter, Tegan, to full term. Our healthy baby girl arrived safely in December 2001, much to our relief and joy

The Journey's destination

Michele's and my far-from-smooth-sailing journey has grown in us both a deep appreciation for life.

It is a possibility that we would never have fully come to know life as the gift that it is, had everything just happened according to "Sean & Michele's Family Plans 101."

Our experience has opened our hearts and peeled back layers of self-sufficiency. There is now a huge dent in our Frank Sinatra, "I did it my way" tendency.

I have always been a make-it-happen kind of guy. Through our losses, I had to come to terms with the fact that I was powerless to make *anything* happen. It was all beyond my control. I could only open myself up to learn and grow through the experience.

Over those four trying years, the thought of using our experience to serve others did not remotely cross Michele's or my mind. We were in no way able to look out beyond our circumstances.

As time passed, however, we began to realize that we had a story to share that could encourage other fellow life travelers.

As a pharmacist, I came into contact with numerous couples struggling to have children (this is more common than ever today) or who were grieving over the loss of a child. Some of these stories were so painful, I could never even attempt to say I entirely understood what they were going through. All I could do was offer an empathetic ear.

Each story made me stop and give thanks for the two little lives we had been given responsibility to parent after five painful losses.

As a result of our experience, Michele and I have made up our minds to become more involved in the lives of orphans.

We have started this ball rolling by sponsoring some children with nutritional products, but we know that there is more waiting for us and for the little lives with whom we will come into contact. In fact, the "more" is shouting out rather loudly.

Our Love Attack journey now involves pursuing ways in which to improve the lives of those little people who most need it, in whichever form or shape seems best, as we live our love lives on the trot.

Love Lives

"Love is growing up."
—James A. Baldwin

Have you ever noticed how we tend to *give* the love that we would like in return from others?

If we like hugs, we give hugs. If we want to be heard, then we engage people in meaningful conversation as often as we can. If we want assurance and affirmation, then we lavish people with words and encouragement.

This means that, for the most part, we are rather selfishly motivated in our demonstrations of "love."

Real love, however, means growing up.

Gone are the days of sitting in the sandpit, shouting and screaming at anyone who dared to want to play with our toys. Loving is learning to give and receive in a mature way.

> **It is imperative that we grow up and become purposeful in our loving.**

It is important in your Love Attack Challenge to figure out your own understanding of love and how you are most likely to show it.

It is also important to find out whether your particular way of showing love actually hits the spot for your loved ones.

The point of the Love Attack, after all, is to see improvement in your love relationships, is it not?

Your Working Definition

You need to have a working definition of what love means for you and your relationships.

By "working definition," I mean a definition that has hands and feet to it—one that is put into action in your love relationships on a daily basis.

Love has legs!

> **If you have no idea what you are aiming for in a loving relationship (i.e., what your target is), then you are bound to miss anything remotely close to it by a mile!**

So give yourself a definition:

1. What do you mean when you tell someone that you love them?

   ____
   ____
   ____
   ____
   ____
   ____

Some of the survey participants gave the following definitions for their understanding of the concept of love:

- "[If I love someone] I want the best for them."
- "[I mean that] you mean a lot to me in my life in whatever role you play."

- "[If I say, 'I love you,' I mean that] I value you. I enjoy being with you. You make me feel safe and happy. You mean more to me than most everybody else with whom I come into contact on a daily basis."
- "[It means that] I see you for who you are and I like what I see".

In the 2004 movie, *Shall We Dance,* Susan Sarandon's character shares poignantly on one of love's realities. She points out that we all want someone to love us because we all need a *witness* to the events that happen in our lives. What we do is given *meaning* if there is someone else to see it and acknowledge it.

On a planet inhabited by billions of people, our loved ones are the ones who promise to be concerned about everything in our lives - a promise essential to our sense of well-being.

From just the above few "definitions," we can see that love is the sum of a number of things. It includes:

- a range of mutually beneficial feelings (enjoyment, acceptance, security, contentment);
- personal intent and action ("I want the best for you");
- a level of value placed on another person ("you mean more to me than …");
- and a level of *need* ("I don't want to be alone").

Do you have your definition?

It is now time to …

Take an Honest Moment

1. How do you show others that you love them?

____

____

____

2. How do you think that others show you that they love you?

3. Do you *feel* loved?

4. Do you think that others feel loved by you?

5. On a scale of 1 to 10, with 1 being "hopeless" and 10 being "Mother Teresa," rate your level of loving:

Once you have finished with the questions above, take your answers to a few of your loved ones and see if they agree with you. Go on, I *dare* you to!

An important ingredient to any loving relationship is communication (more on this later), so you might as well take the plunge and get that ball rolling.

Mind the Gap

There are often gaps between how we think we are performing in our love relationships and how others might actually be receiving us.

Let's call this the broken telephone[25] of loving communication.

For example, you might be happily cooking, cleaning, or hanging pictures, because that is how you show others that you care for them, while your husband or wife would *much* prefer you to be sharing time and conversation with them at that rugby game or over a candlelit dinner!

Your son or daughter might simply be longing for you to give them a hug or to speak kindly to them, but instead you buy toys and gadgets for their enjoyment because *you* love it when people buy *you* gifts.

If you want to see improvement in your love relationships, you will need to work on narrowing these gaps.

Spend some more time asking your loved ones the following questions:

1. How can I walk my love talk today? (Actions do speak louder than words!)

---

25 We have probably all played the "broken telephone" game as children, or something similar to it. Here children sit in a circle and wait for a message that is being passed down the line to be whispered into their ears. The rules of the game state that you pass along what you hear without being able to confirm it with anyone back up the line. The message is normally accompanied by a fair deal of puzzled looks on faces, "Pardons?" and some spit. By the time the message gets back to its originator, it is considerably different from how it started out, might be a bit rude (as some children go), and has everyone in hysterics.

2. Is there anything I'm doing that is limiting or hindering our love flow?

3. I want each day to be a new love day. Will you tell me if I've hit the mark?

   Write down their answers. Read them and "chew" on them.

   Can you feel that cannibal called Selfishness rising up within you as you contemplate putting their answers into action? I know that it does for me!

   Oftentimes, we would like to be back in the sandpit at playschool,[26] secure in the knowledge that the world revolves around *us* and therefore will not make too many demands of our time and energies.

   It is true that love does not make us a doormat; nor does it turn us into someone to be used and abused by others.

   Giving and showing love, however, does take a concerted effort. You will only get out what you put into your relationships. You reap what you sow—this is a fact!

> **We have to whip our love worlds into shape and break into a sweat if we want to become people who truly love.**

The Seven-Day Love Challenge

How about setting yourself a **Seven-Day Love Challenge?**

Set apart the next seven days to intentionally demonstrate your love to your family members and friends in ways that you know will have meaning to them.

At the end of each day, record:

---

26 Crèche, pre-primary school.

- How you feel after having purposefully worked on your levels of loving;
- Any positive change that you can see in your relationships;
- Anything else that I have not suggested you record that you would like to add. (This is *your* love journey, after all!)

I would suggest that for best results, you go about the Seven-Day Love Challenge as subtly as you can.

Don't send your girlfriend a bunch of flowers with a small note attached that reads, "You told me that you would like me to give you flowers, so here they are."

That will just kill the romance. No one likes to think that their loved ones merely love them out of a sense of obligation.

Have fun with this challenge. Get creative!

Don't consider it a one-off thing either. The point is to make loving a natural part of your life. The Seven-Day Love Challenge is just a tool to get the ball rolling.

THE LOVE ATTACK CHALLENGE:

The Three Cs

"Give back better than you are given."
—Dr. Henry Cloud

I propose the Three Cs of *communication*, *choice,* and *change* as three vital, supportive "legs" for all relationships.

C #1: Communication

Consider the following scenario.

You and your loved one are growing increasingly more snappish and irritable around each other. There is trouble in the love jungle.

You know that you both need to sit down and have it out with one another.

You need to figure out why you are both offended, and then you need to figure out a way of constructively resolving this offense.

The problem is that it is *far* easier to skirt around a problem or avoid the issue altogether than to face it and another person head-on!

- You rush off to bed to escape what you fear will be a communication lockdown, instead of purposefully lingering around to bring up an issue with your wife.

  Maybe if you avoid the issue it will just go away, right?

- You make excuses to your mother-in-law about busy schedules, to avoid having to pop in for tea and a needed chat.
- You smile awkwardly across the office at a colleague with whom you are clashing and then make a quick duck into the restroom or pretend to be on an urgent call until they have (hopefully) moved off elsewhere.

For many, direct communication and confrontation is a highly uncomfortable thing.

We worry that confronting an issue in a relationship will make the relationship worse instead of better.

We might feel inadequate in our ability to express our thoughts and emotions.

We might dislike making ourselves vulnerable through honest communication.

We might have grown up in a family that avoided communication and confrontation and so were never taught healthy ways of raising and resolving issues.

There are reasons a-plenty for all of our poor communication skills. However, none of them is good enough if we want to make our relationships work.

The Greek philosopher, Socrates, once pointed out that "the unexamined life is not worth living."

Communication is a part of life. We need to ensure that our *love lives* are worth living.

We all need to examine ourselves and ask ourselves many "why" and "how" questions regarding the way that we communicate and engage with others.

Owning the ways that you communicate and the ways in which you might fail to communicate is a step towards growing up in your levels of loving.

Take Off the Tinted Glasses

When it comes to successful communication, it is important to realize that individuals look at their world and relationships through a *biased* grid of experience.

Imagine that from infancy onwards, you were given a unique pair of glasses to wear each day.

These glasses may have started out crystal clear, but over time, have developed a dark tint to their lenses.

This tint comes from the judgments that you have made about yourself, relationships, and life based on everything you have seen, heard, and experienced over the years.

What is more, everything that you currently understand and perceive gets filtered through the tint of these glasses.

If your mother is more of a demanding "sergeant major" type, for example, then you might automatically approach other older women as cautiously and respectfully as you would approach her.

They might be warm, inviting, and harmless, but it is hard for you to trust this because your lenses allow you to see only one thing as you engage with them—your scary mother!

Knowing the particular "tint" of your lenses will help you understand any defensiveness or unhealthy expectations that you might have as you communicate with your loved ones.

Understanding the particular tint of your loved ones' lenses (taking into consideration their histories, personalities, and the unique characteristics of their gender) will also help you in your communication.

Communication is not about steamrolling over your loved ones with your opinions and perspectives. Nor is communication about being *right*. How can anyone be completely right when we are all so biased?

Communication is about trying your best to understand another person in order to reach happy middle ground in the relationship.

Some Self-Examination ...

It is time to pull your glasses off and give them a good inspection, in order to understand your communication style better.

Ask yourself the following questions:

- How do I express my thoughts, emotions, and opinions?
- Do I keep them to myself?
- Do I let issues build until I finally, inexplicably explode?
- Do I drop hints instead of taking the direct approach?
- Do I expect my loved ones to somehow sniff out what might be wrong with me by my behavior alone?
- Do I vent my frustrations to other people who I know will support me in my opinions?
- Do I take time to process my emotions and reactions and then verbalize them in an appropriate and constructive way?
- Do I sulk and hope that my pity party will somehow evoke love from another?
- How and where did I learn to communicate?

Think about who your role models have been—your parent(s), your peers, teachers, work colleagues, the media.

What have you picked up from them in the way that you now relate to and communicate with other people?

Do you think that your role models were helpful or harmful to how you presently communicate with others?

For example, did the environment in which you grew up encourage free, honest, and safe communication, or were you made to feel bad about having an opinion different from that of your family?

If the latter was the case, you might now struggle to share honestly in your current love relationships, for fear of having your feelings squashed or trampled on. You might not even value your own opinion!

Perhaps you grew up in a home where flying fists, shouting, and arguments were the norm. You have learned to *fight* to get your way, and loved ones now struggle to approach you to communicate, for fear of having their heads bitten off.

The reality is that much of what you were taught and have caught regarding communication probably needs a major facelift!

Many of us were modeled immature ways of communicating—from laying on the silent treatment thick and fast, to plate-throwing sessions, to blame-shifting or manipulation.

We have to learn to separate ourselves from any negative forms of communication that we have picked up from our childhood.

We need to learn to make more constructive decisions regarding how we express our opinions, needs, desires, and emotions if we want our love relationships to improve.

Another Important Question to Ask Yourself:

- Do I take time to truly *listen* to my loved ones, or am I only interested in being heard and having my feelings and opinions affirmed and validated?

This question reminds me of an amusing commercial that I saw on television. In the commercial, we find a very talkative, elderly wife jabbering away to her elderly husband in the car. By facial expressions alone (because he has no chance to get a word in edgewise), you can tell that the old man is fairly used to humoring his wife's chattering. You can also tell that he needs a break!

At one point, we see his face light up happily: he has spotted the turnoff to his favorite coffee shop. The next clip of the commercial shows them seated in the shop, with the wife still jabbering away into his one ear.

There is suddenly a long silence. The husband smiles in a very pleased manner, and the camera pans over to his now speechless wife sipping her coffee. Finally, for the old man, a minute's peace (thanks to the franchise's fabulous specialty coffee, of course).

Although the commercial uses stereotypes about the feminine trend to overly communicate and the masculine trend to keep thoughts in reserve, it does bring me to my next point: **Communication is as much about listening as it is about being heard.**

Active Listening

Chaps, what I mean by *active listening* is this:

Maintain eye contact and throw away the TV remote or your favorite gadget of choice that would distract you from what your loved one is trying to tell you.

(Active listening is *not* gazing over the top of your laptop at your wife with one eye while scanning your e-mails with the other!)

Ask questions or make statements that *show* that you have been listening:

"How do you feel about that?"

"What can I do to help you?"

Or

"I can see that you are angry (sad, frustrated, confused) about this …"

"That must have been difficult for you."

"That is great!"

Ladies, how about truly focusing on what your loved one is saying, instead of running your responses through your head about half a sentence into the conversation?

I once had the experience of sitting across from someone who spent at least half of the conversation (my half!) silently mouthing the words that he wanted to say in answer to my story!

At one point, I wondered if I should just shut up and let this person have his say. To be honest, I am not even sure if he would have noticed!

Lastly, when communicating, avoid dead-end questions that can easily be answered with a short, sharp "Yes!" or a grunt or two.

If your loved ones struggle to communicate as it is, asking them an "Are you all right?" type of question won't get you very far down the road with them in a meaningful heart-to-heart.

C #2: Choice

Our ability to *choose* is a key aspect of our loving relationships.

Love is more of a choice than any of us would like to admit.

> **We choose on a daily basis to love those around us, or we choose not to. It's as simple as that.**

We don't often realize it, but saying *yes* to someone or something means we are also, by definition, saying *no* to someone or something else.

For example, if I choose to stay on and do paperwork at the office rather than get home on time to sit and have a meal with my family, this essentially means that I am saying yes to my desires and no to those of my family.

That is my choice, and I have made it.

The "Tyranny of the Urgent"

We often believe that those things we choose above our love relationships are things that "just *have* to be done." Work demands are often placed above our family's need for our time and attention because money, deadlines, and bosses are involved, which makes them "urgent."

What would the consequences be if you simply choose to live the *important* rather than the urgent?

Urgency speeds up our pace and our anxieties and eats away at our availability. We become preoccupied with whatever we perceive to be urgent, and we lose our ability to be present to what is actually important.

On the other hand, if we focus on what *is* important, then we can invariably slow our lives down and learn to protect and love what is actually valuable and good for us.

> **Ask yourself this crucial question:**
>
> **What and whom do I value?**

I remember reading an article in a pharmaceutical magazine a few years ago featuring interviews with terminally ill and elderly *hospice* patients.

They were asked what they would do differently if they were given the opportunity to live their lives over again. I noted that not a single man or woman mentioned the desire to spend more time at work!

Rather, they regretted the time that they had spent on *other* activities when they could have been with their loved ones.

In the preface of Philip Yancey's book, *Soul Survivor,* he tells of the sobering effect that the events of September 11, 2001 had on the American nation as a whole: "That three thousand people could go to work as part of their daily routine and never come home made us all aware of our fragile mortality."[27]

According to Yancey, with this newfound awareness came a "massive shift in perspective." He shares that many Americans learned that day, among other things, that "playing games with kids may be more important than working late for overtime pay."

It would be tragic for any of us to reach the end of our lives with the regretful realization that we have spent more time on "to dos," projects, and things than with the people who matter most to us.

Note to self: spend more time with the people I love!

Making a difference starts with a choice and ends with an action!

The key is to choose change in our love lives and then to become *intentional* in making that change happen.

Here are a few more examples of using your ability to choose well in a relationship.

"Positive Speak"

British orator, author, and prime minister, Winston Churchill, once said that "[w]e are masters of the unsaid words, but slaves of those we let slip out."[28]

Few of us understand the power of the spoken word.

According to an ancient proverb, the power of life and death is in the tongue.[29]

27 Yancey, Philip. 2003. *Soul Survivor.* Waterbrook Press, USA. p. xvii and xv.
28 www.ThinkExist.com.
29 Proverbs 18:21.

Think on things said about your character, personality, appearance, or performance in your own lifetime.

How did it feel when someone gave you genuine praise and affirmation? Did it feel like "soul food"?

What about those *negative* statements that came your way? I am pretty sure that they stole the wind out of your sails and killed your self-confidence, self-esteem, and joy.

You see, words have power to create or to destroy.

Have a look at the following negative statements.

"I nearly died."

"I could have *killed* him!"

"I absolutely *hate* ...!"

"I have a feeling that this is going to be a *disaster*."

"So-and-so drives me *mad!*"

"He cannot do *anything* right!"

If we lived as if the words we speak had the power to do what we said the minute they left our mouths, might we choose our words a bit more carefully?

What if you chose to speak positively about your loved ones—both to their faces and about them when they are not around?

How could your choosing to voice your positive views change both the way that they think about themselves and about you?

But what if there is nothing positive to say? I hear you ask.

FIND IT!

Search for the smallest, seemingly insignificant, positive trait/talent/gift/ability and focus on that!

Your husband may not be doing an excellent job of loving you right now, but he may be an excellent handyman. Compliment him on a job well done, and tell him how much you appreciate him hanging the pictures. Then watch the changes that take place!

Your sullen teenager might give you the impression that she wants nothing to do with the good things that you have to say about her. You are her "outdated" parent, after all, so what would you know?

It is a lie! She needs you. Affirm her anyway!

We live in an overly negative world. We often fail to have enough grace or space for ourselves or for each other.

> **If our loved ones do not receive positive affirmation from us, then they might just look for it in other places—often to their own detriment.**

Do you want your love relationships to be characterized by criticism or loving affirmation?

It is your choice.

"Positive Seek"

"He who walks with the wise grows wise, but a companion of fools suffers harm."[30]

Wherever possible, choose to spend your life with positive people and make a constructive contribution to their lives.

I might extend my hand to a negative person to pull him onto my Life Boat for a short trip around the bay, but I definitely would not choose

30 Proverbs 13:20.

to go on a long journey with him if he insists on constantly feeding and expressing his negativity.

Michele and I choose to hang with positive people as often as we can. One place we do this is in a networking company we have joined whose products have greatly influenced our health.

Every time we return from a conference or training, we feel renewed and revived by just having hung out with people who focus on solutions rather than on problems.

Wow, what a difference this has made!

If I can encourage you to do anything, I would say this—find a group, organization, church, or tribe that is all about adding value, serving, and encouraging others, and join it.

It will change your life!

C#2: Change

"I wish you would not …"

"I wish you were more …"

"Can you not just …"

For our worlds to run as smoothly as we would like them to, we know that our loved ones need to change.

After all, it is in *their* behavior and attitudes that most of our problems lie, is it not?

They might not give us enough of their time. They might not understand us as well as we think they could. They might need to work on their tone when they speak to us, their levels of defensiveness, or their unrealistic demands or helpfulness in general.

The lists of how your loved ones could improve are probably endless, I know. (I am pulling your leg here!)

Most of us know the answers to most relational problem questions, understand the theory of really loving and could (and do) lecture our partners on the specifics needed for them to change for everything to be fine.

The reality is that, "for things to change, I must change."

Change Starts with *You*!

As Cloud and Townsend point out, growing relationships are made up of "growing people."[31]

The opposite is true: stagnant relationships are made up of stagnant people who refuse to change.

Albert Einstein once said that a mark of insanity is "doing the same things over and over again and expecting different results"[32].

(If that is the case, then we are probably all a bit insane!)

It's like walking a well-known trail in a forest and stubbornly refusing to duck your head when you reach a low-hanging branch that you have walked into countless times before.

Would anyone in their right mind do that? No!

Then why do we insist on sticking to our attitudes, approaches, and behavioral patterns that have failed countless times and caused harm in our love relationships?

My Own Change Challenge

I love to talk! I love to tell a story and make people laugh.

The problem with this enthusiasm is that I can oftentimes get so excited about a story that I jump in and take over when Michele is sharing her version of it.

---

31 Cloud, Dr. Henry & Townsend, Dr. John. 2005. *Rescue Your Love Life*. Nashville, Tenn.: Integrity Publishers, p. 5.

32 http://www.brainyquote.com/quotes

What a disaster!

For the first few years of our marriage, my beautiful wife never said how this habit of mine irritated the life out of her. I'm not sure when she eventually did tell me how she felt, and I'm not sure how long it took for me to realize just how rude it was to think that I could hijack the conversation in my zeal to add some "spice" to the story.

All I know is that we spoke about it, and it has been (and still is) an ongoing decision that I now make *not* to interrupt her or speak over her.

Do I always get this right? Definitely not!

Because of our love journey, she now lets me know right then and there in her loving way that I "missed it."

I had to choose to change—not an easy or comfortable thing to do, but a choice that I wanted to make because I knew that this would take our love relationship to a whole new level.

Another example of having to choose to change comes to mind.

I used to be a very reactive person. When I heard Michele getting angry because the kids had done something to upset her, I would come out from wherever I was in the house with my guns blazing, almost steaming from both ears.

I can think of a few times when I really lost it with my children and where I threatened to "knock them into next week." I deeply regretted the words I used and the emotions I expressed.

Things *had* to change, and for things to change, I had to change!

I decided to set my intention to *respond* rather than react, and although I still don't always respond exactly the way I'd like to (it's a journey, after all), I love the new "road less travelled."

Abraham Maslow said, "You will either step forward into growth, or you will step backward into safety."[33]

Choose growth!

---

33 http://en.wikiquote.org/wiki/Abraham_Maslow.

THE LOVE ATTACK CHALLENGE:

Gratitude Journal

"Reason demands moderation in love as in all things, but faith destroys moderation here. Faith tolerates a moderate love of one's fellow man no more than it tolerates a moderate love between God and man."

—John McKenzie

I have said it before, and I will say it again: we need to get intentional in making our love lives happen.

I have already suggested the **Seven-Day Love Challenge** as a means for you to do this.

Another way to keep your life love levels on the healthy "up" is to keep a Gratitude Journal.

I like to spend a few minutes of each day quietly contemplating and recording the good things that have happened in that day. I include the specific reasons why I might be thankful for a significant person in my life.

These I write down in my Gratitude Journal.

To give you an idea of what you can include in your Gratitude Journal, have a look at my gratitude thoughts over the last week.

These thoughts encompass my whole family and some life experiences.

Wednesday, 1st December:

Tonight it's hard to explain just how incredibly proud I am of Tegan—from a little girl who wouldn't look up in school concerts to a solo performance in the Paarl Theatre tonight; what a mighty leap outside her comfort zone! I am grateful that I was there to witness this HUGE step of faith ...

Thursday, 2nd December:

What an awesome day! Nathan had his prize-giving and walked away with the top English spot and also a Merit Certificate! I am blessed once again!

Friday, 3rd December:

Mom is staying with us for the week, and she read my draft of the book—she was blown away and told me how proud my dad would have been—I am so grateful for my eighty-one-year-old mom!

Saturday, 4th December:

Today was Gazza and Fran's wedding—I am grateful for the incredible weather, the gathering of our entire family for this occasion, for my mom to witness her first grandchild's wedding, and for Michele's reassuring hand (more to follow)!

Sunday, 5th December:

Last night I hardly slept, concerned that the video footage I had been charged with taking at the wedding had been completely lost—the video showed "disc error." Michele reassured me that all would work out well ... what an amazing wife and lady she is!

Today we managed to salvage a large part of the video—wow, I am thankful!

Monday, 6th December:

Today I played Dad's taxi and loved it! I'm so blessed to have two amazing kids!

Tuesday, 7th December:

I was on a conference call and Michele quietly brought me a cup of tea—

how often hasn't she done that … how often doesn't she just quietly spoil me … I am so blessed!

Wednesday, 8th December:

Today I called a friend to ask about a pharmacy-related question, and he mentioned I should call someone about my book. .

It turns out Gus is also a cartoonist! I am so grateful for the doors that are opening for my book and the people I'm meeting on the journey!

Thursday, 9th December:

Michele and I had a ball today at the shops, ending with supper at the V & A Waterfront and some wonderful conversation! She helps me to live in the moment …

> Writing these little observations down each day helps me to continue looking for the best in my loved ones. My eyes become accustomed to looking for the positive things about life.

This is a much better alternative to keeping my attention fixed on life's or my loved ones' shortcomings!

Remember, "What you focus on the longest becomes the strongest."

Feed what is good in your relationships by choosing to stubbornly fix your gaze on the positive things that they bring you.

THE LOVE ATTACK CHALLENGE:

Conclusion

A Love Attack begins with an intention that then needs to be acted upon to make it worthwhile.

"I am going to look for every excuse I can find in the day to be grateful for my lovely wife." Nice!

The above is a stated intention that won't just naturally happen unless you develop a plan of action to *make* sure that it does.

You will need to move past the "thinking, scheming, and dreaming" of your Love Attack if you want to see any change take place.

I am sure that there are other Love Attack triggers—dozens even—that I and others could suggest for you to begin your journey.

In this section of the book, I have recommended that you take the **Seven-Day Love Challenge** and that you start a **Gratitude Journal** in order to stoke and feed your love levels.

If all you do in the next three months are these two things, I know that your love life will be forever changed.

"A person without a sense of humor is like a wagon without springs. It's jolted by every pebble on the road."

—Henry Ward Beecher

THE LAUGH ATTACK CHALLENGE

Planet Mirth ...

"The most thoroughly wasted of all days is that on which one has not laughed."
—Chamfort

Once upon a time, there was a planet of people bobbing around on their Life Boats. These people never *ever* laughed or smiled.

People on this world were *very* serious, because obviously, Life Boat matters are such serious matters and nobody could afford to crack a smile.

All you could hear each day, drifting across the water, was the sound of the toiling, complaining, sighing, and arguing going on aboard each Life Boat.

The occupants of this world were not only severe, they were also tired and stressed out. All their grimness had made them a rather sick bunch, which made them unpleasant company for anyone visiting from other planets.

There were never too many visitors, and those who did pop in left sooner than planned, with excuses about irons left on at home by mistake, shopping to be done, kids needing to be collected, and mothers-in-law needing to be visited.

One day, however, a little child tripped on one of the Life Boat decks. He had been carefully and soberly carrying dessert to the dinner table and had forgotten to look where he was going.

The three-tiered chocolate cake teetered for a second and then toppled overboard onto a low-flying and unsuspecting sea bird.

For some reason, he found this rather funny.

This little boy's mother found him leaning over the boat rail, guffawing into the water below and was so overcome with his glee that she began to laugh too.

Very soon, everyone in this Life Boat was leaning up against furniture, masts, cabin windows, or over railings, caught up in a good belly laugh and wiping merry tears from their eyes. No one seemed to mind that they were now out of pudding.

Even the seagulls above their heads began to squawk with joy, and the sea creatures that had been sullenly slinking along below the water's surface popped up to the top to have a look and a relieved chuckle.

People on this Life Boat felt strangely lighter once they were done with their laughing. Some even began to sing merry tunes as they went about the rest of their day.

Over the next few weeks, they began to look for opportunities to have a good chuckle—over odd hairstyles, funny things said or done, and the like.

It soon became quite a regular sight to spot someone on the Life Boat stopping his work to give a funny moment his full attention and energy.

This now-happy Life Boat became *the* Life Boat with which to be seen sharing water space.

It was not long before unneeded seriousness was banished from the waters surrounding many Life Boats, and within a few months, this once-severe planet became a favorite holiday destination for all weary travelers needing to relax, unwind, and experience the lighter side of life.

The inhabitants of this once-unhappy planet regretted all the time that they had given to being so somber, and so as never to return to that unhappy state, renamed their world "Planet Mirth."

Enjoying the Journey

"Pure and simple, any person who is enjoying life is a success."
—William Feather

To have a Laugh Attack is to find oneself "elbows deep" in the enjoyment of life.

People who enjoy life are *active* participants in their own circumstances and realities. You won't find them sitting in the grandstands, yawning and passing commentary about the game below.

No, they will be deep in the thick of it, guffawing loudly and infecting others with their unreserved delight.

We all take pleasure in people who have the capacity to enjoy life, so my question to you today is this: *why contain the humour?*

- Are you caught up in dusty respectability?
- Are you more of a melancholic, "glass-half-empty" kind of person?
- Are you in "victim mode," handing over your power to people and events to let *them* dictate to *you* how much of your life you can spend having a blast?
- Are you waiting for the "right" or "perfect" circumstances before you will fully commit to having a laugh at life?

The fascinating reality about living is that, other than *now,* there is no such thing as the "right" or "perfect" time to enjoy it.

Many a happy person has discovered that life is best laughed at when a few odds are stacked against them.

So, tell me, what are your reasons for being so grim?

Would you like to list them here … and then *let go of them?*

If you are currently weighed down by responsibility, conflict, demands, and worries, then the best medicine that I can recommend is for you to have a hearty and long belly laugh!

If you are reading this book, I'm going to assume that you are alive. Please tell me now if you are not, so we can call a paramedic! If you *are* going to live, why not choose to do so with daily doses of humour and laughter?

In these next few chapters, I will give you good reasons why laughter is *the* 4x4 vehicle that you should use for your Life Attack ride.

THE LAUGH ATTACK CHALLENGE

Does a spoonful of laughter make your medicine bill go down?

"We must laugh before we are happy, for fear we die before we laugh at all."

—Jean de la Fontain

Disease is often just that: a *lack* of ease.

Stress, fear, and anxiety account for many of the health complaints (migraine headaches, muscle tension, high blood pressure, heart attacks, strokes, and even some forms of cancer) that highly strung members of planet Earth experience today.

Our bodies are in constant reaction to our environments. We absorb information through our senses throughout the day that then gets carried to our brain for our conscious or subconscious response.

> Oftentimes, our response to all this information is a *stress* response.

As our stress levels increase, our breathing deepens and quickens, our muscles tense, and we start to use our upper chest area to breathe instead of our belly.[34]

Doing all of this sends signals to our brains that we are in *distress*.

This distress triggers our bodies to release more adrenaline, the hormone that prepares us to respond to danger.

34 Peurifoy, Reneau Z., 2005. *Anxiety, Phobias and Panic: A Step by Step Programme for Regaining Control of Your Life.* London: Piatkus, pp. 5–6.

As our adrenaline levels increase, our bodies get primed with enough muscle alertness and energy to give the perceived threat a solid *belting,* or to turn around and hightail it out of there (if this seems the wiser option).

This is called the body's "fight or flight" response.[35]

More often than not, our day-to-day "threats" are *psychological,* which means that we cannot necessarily run away or release our inner Karate Kid.

Prolonged stress and anxiety introduce more adrenaline into our bodies than needed, which suppresses our immune systems, increases our blood pressure, and drains our humour reserves down to near empty.

It is quite clear—for the sake of our health and wellness—we need to take charge of our stress levels.

Happy People Are Healthy People

Much research has been done into establishing the positive effects of a healthy and active "funny bone."

According to Dr. William Fry, associate professor of clinical psychiatry at Stanford University, regular laughing sessions increase the heart rate, improve blood circulation, and work muscles all over the body.[36]

Just think about the last time you had a side-splitting, floor-rolling laughter session. How did you feel afterward? Pleasantly relaxed? More carefree? Were your stomach muscles happily complaining?

Laughter is a great form of stress relief. It actually *inhibits* our fight-or-flight response—which helps our bodies to wind down and relax.[37]

---

35 Ibid.

36 Puder, C. (1998). The healthful effects of laughter. *Journal of Child and Youth Care.* Vol.12 No.3 pp 45-53

37 http://www.wellsphere.com/mind-body-article/healing-effects-of-laughter

Studies have also revealed that the health benefits of laughter range from a strengthened immune system[38] to an increased threshold for pain. As we laugh, our bodies release natural painkillers called endorphins into our systems. Endorphins are also great combatants against depression.[39]

On top of all of these many benefits to a healthy sense of humour, an active laugh life also motivates us positively and improves our overall sense of well-being.

On the strength of these findings alone, it is clear that we need as many endorphins racing through our systems as possible. We need to get to laughing!

Laughter Therapy

Hospital-based child life specialist Christine Puder has seen firsthand the benefits of introducing humour and regular "belly laughing" sessions into the healing environment.

In her article, "The Healthful Effects of Laughter," Puder shares that regular doses of humour, used in connection with conventional, medical treatment, are known to improve pain tolerance and reduce pain levels in adult arthritis and cancer patients.[40]

This therapeutic approach is widely known as Laughter Therapy.

Kids get sick too, so Puder introduced Laughter Therapy into a child life department she was administrating—with positive results!

Humour rooms (stocked with all things funny, like comics, cartoon strips, funny posters, and funny audiotapes and videos), humour carts (humour rooms on wheels for kids unable to get out of bed), clown care programs, and happy hours are now the order of the day!

You can imagine that a laughing child has less time to be anxious about his or her illness or to feel lonely or depressed.

---

38 http://www.wellsphere.com/mind-body-article/healing-effects-of-laughter

39 Puder, C. (1998). The healthful effects of laughter. *Journal of Child and Youth Care.* Vol.12 No.3 pp 45-53

40 Puder, C. (1998). The healthful effects of laughter. *Journal of Child and Youth Care.* Vol.12 No.3 pp 45-53

An environment that intentionally finds ways to increase happiness levels is probably a great place to be for staff and visitors too.

One organization, Cancer Treatment Centers of America (CTCA), runs therapy sessions with its patients called Laughter Clubs or Humour Groups.[41]

These clubs are different to Puder's humour rooms in that they use laughter as a *physical* exercise. Patients meet as a group and go through a series of laughter exercises demonstrated to them by a group leader.

Try this one on for size:

Place your fingertips on your cheekbones, chest, or lower abdomen and make "ha ha" or "hee hee" sounds. Feel the vibrations of these sounds through your body.

As you *mimic* laughter reflexes in this way, you will be receiving all the good aftereffects of a genuine laugh. And because you might feel a bit silly or find the exercise amusing, it might turn into a genuine belly laugh!

Now add a *bunch* of people to the mix, all "ha ha-ing" and "hee hee-ing," and tell me that you won't soon be cracking up with laughter.

Patch Adams

These "healthful" effect of laughter that Puder (and many others) have discovered in the medical profession, reminds me of the 1998 movie, *Patch Adams*, starring actor-comedian Robin Williams.

Based on a true story, this motion picture tells the tale of a middle-aged man living in the 1960s who discovers the benefits of humour in the most unlikely of places.

Patch finds himself in a "dark wood" of depression and commits himself into a psychiatric hospital as he becomes increasingly suicidal.

He finds the institution and its staff to be clinical and indifferent to his pain. He and the other psychiatric patients are treated more as

41 http://www.cancercenter.com/

problems than as human beings, and very little is done to address their true psychological needs.

As a naturally funny guy, Patch begins to use humour to lighten the mood in group counseling sessions, which proves to be very effective in getting the other patients to open up and begin to bond with each other.

In one hilarious scene in the movie, Patch helps his roommate overcome his fear of imaginary squirrels by entering into his world of dread and introducing make-believe handguns, rifles, and bazookas to eliminate the "squirrel infestation."

As the two men laugh and play like very big children, his roommate's trepidation is dispelled; he no longer feels *alone* in his fear, and his anxieties are diminished by looking at them through a funnier lens.

Very soon, Patch's sense of purpose and enjoyment of life returns as he realizes that he can both connect to people and help them by making them chuckle. He also discovers that *his* problems begin to fade into the background as he focuses on helping others laugh at their own troubles.

Patch now knows that he wants to spend his life adding joy to the lives of people in need. He decides to attend a medical university to become a doctor.

Very soon, we find him introducing his unorthodox medical approach into the university-based hospital, clowning around in the children's oncology wards, and helping elderly and terminal patients live out their childhood fantasies and dreams.

When challenged on his approach (as he is throughout the movie), he points out that treating an illness alone means that if nothing improves, then everyone loses. If you treat a patient and *connect* in relationship to a patient, Patch adds that even if there is no improvement in the person's health, everyone still wins.

The *real* Patch Adams, Hunter Adams, on whose life and experience the movie is based, is as eccentric a character as the one that Robin Williams acts in the movie.

In one interview, Hunter sports a theatrical moustache that curls up at the edges, and he wears a small table fork as an earring in one ear! His clothes are bright and gaudy, and he has a blue streak in his ponytailed hair. He is intensely passionate about keeping life and medicine both funny *and* honest.

He believes that laughter and humour create a spontaneous joy, which provides a great climate in which to do any healing. He enjoys the notion of humour being used to prevent burnout in individuals working in the helping profession.

A Comedian's Take on Laughter

One of my mentors, Sandy Griffin, from Nashville, Tennessee, recently interviewed her Russian comedian friend, Yakov Smirnoff, for this funny fellow's take on life, love and laughter. She has kindly allowed me to share a few nuggets from that interview with you.

Comedian, painter, and teacher Yakov Smirnoff was born and raised in Ukraine in the Soviet Union.

To give you an idea about the political and social climate of the Soviet Union during his childhood, here is a quote from America's fortieth president, Ronald Reagan, on the subject:

> "It is the Soviet Union that runs against the tide of human history by denying human freedom and human dignity to its citizens."[42]

Yakov shares that a person could choose to relieve the tension of growing up in this "not so funny place to live" by either laughing or crying about it.

> "[V]ery much like a funeral, after the grieving, you have to laugh and giggle … there is a desire to laugh in these sad environments because laughter releases tension."

42 www.ThinkExist.com.

Yakov chose to have a good chuckle, and found that from a young age, he had the knack of helping others do the same.

He sees it as a gift to help others laugh and his experience is that people seek out the comic relief he provides them *especially* when the going is tough.

He believes that:

> "it is easier to laugh when life is challenging because there is such a need for it. With me, the more problems I have, the more I release my humor on people. I believe everyone has this capacity."

When asked by Sandy Griffin what advice he would give to people about adding fun to their lives, he shared that he has noted over the years that those who *naturally* entertain and those who seek out entertainment actually have the same need—to be relieved of their tension.

He believes that we should all find those people who add laughter to our hearts because we will be happier for it!

If you consider that laughter is organic, *free,* can be administered with no side effects (except for possibly wetting oneself), and is endorsed by the medical professional and *all* comedians, then I can see no reason for delay.

We need to get to laughing!

The Shortest Distance ...

"Laughter is the sun that drives winter from the human face."
—Victor Hugo

Laughter is not only good medicine; it can also bring people together.

If you were a fly on a wall at any social gathering, what key elements would you notice most?

Talking, yes; food and drink, for sure; the usual levels of apprehension, of course; but *always* laughter.

A good number of researchers believe that one of laughter's purposes is related to making and strengthening our human connections.[43]

We often use laughter to ease social awkwardness or to create a sense of belonging in a group. Laughter signals acceptance and shows that there are positive interactions going on among people in a room.[44]

Having a giggle, chuckle, chortle, squeal, or guffaw with others melts away social barriers and helps everyone uncross their arms, loosen their ties, let their hair down, and move beyond their social clique.

> It is noteworthy that the shortest distance between any two people is a laugh.[45]

43 http://health.howstuffworks.com/mental-health/human-nature/other-emotions/laughter.htm/.

44 http://en.wikipedia.org/wiki/Laughter.

45 Victor Borge in www.ThinkExist.com.

The tension in any argument will often be defused if someone says or does something funny.

Laughter offers us both emotional and physical relief in the heat of conflict, giving us opportunity to *breathe* and to glimpse the lighter side of our relationships.

And it *always* helps to see the funnier side of our relationships …

So I ask you:

Are you feeling estranged from a loved one?

Are you battling to make friends?

Can you not seem to relate to people at work?

Is your teenager frosting you out with cold, accusatory glares?

Laugh!

> **You might be pointing at yourself, shouting, "Please help! I think I lost my sense of humour!"**

In fact, those with whom you come in contact on a daily basis might be nodding their heads in silent agreement, just *longing* for you to crack a smile sometime this century.

It is actually easier to find a mislaid sense of humour than you think. Life is *teeming* with opportunity to have a giggle.

Why not make a list of fifty things regarding your life, work, and relationships that you could laugh about on a daily basis?

Maybe your car is so old that it is falling to pieces around you—what a *great* source of entertainment!

Or your elderly father has just moved into your tiny home with you and your family. What a hoot!

Do your pets do funny things—like chase their own tails, or lie on their backs, spread-eagled, without a care in the world?

What about the people driving in the cars around you on your way to work? Are they in any way funny?

A Funny Five

Why not try introducing a **Funny Five** into the time that you spend with your loved ones or peers?

Family members or digs mates, couples, or close friends—any group of people, really— can *only* benefit from spending five minutes together each day, telling a joke, a funny story, or sharing an amusing experience that they have had in the day.

> **Being overly serious and severe about our lives and relationships is never going to *improve* them.**

You might be facing a very grim reality at the moment—a death in the family, a nasty divorce, estrangement from a loved one, or hurtful conflict in the workplace.

At the end of the day, there are many things over which we have no control. We might as well learn to laugh about them!

There is a saying that a young friend of mine has used as a reminder to seek out fun and enjoyment in her life despite her grief over a miscarriage and the loss of her two beloved sons shortly after their births:

"Pleasure races pain to the brain."

If you *intentionally* do those things that you enjoy and that make you laugh and feel good about yourself, then your pain will be forced to register second, rather than first, in your brain's gray matter.

Pleasure *overrides* pain. Endorphins *override* fatigue and anxiety.

In doing this, you are essentially giving your body a fighting chance to recover emotionally from the stress and strain of your experiences.

So, be kind to yourself and have a giggle!

Happy Humour Hour

"Did you hear about the duck that walked into the pharmacy and asked for a painkiller? The pharmacist said, 'Sure! Will that be cash?' The duck answered, 'Nah, just put it on my bill!'"

—Anonymous

When was the last time that you took your insides jogging at your workplace?

Our work environments do not have to be half as serious as we make them!

If you are in agreement, then why not introduce a Happy Humour Hour onto the work week to-do list to lighten the tension and keep work stress at bay?

Gather the working troops for an hour each week with the sole intention of having a laugh.

Ideas to get you started:

- Share your funniest life experiences with each other;
- Watch funny videos;
- Vote for the office's "funniest moment of the week," including a prize for the best story.
- Bring your baby pictures to work and have a competition to guess whose picture is whose.

- Bring your photographs from the '80s and have a good laugh at them during your Happy Humour Hour.

Why not create a space in your workplace designed to give your colleagues a good chuckle?

You could:

- Devote a coffee table to comic books;
- Set aside a section of a bulletin/notice board for funny pictures, weekly jokes, and comic strips;
- Create a humour room or corner where somberness, criticism, or pessimism is strictly prohibited.

> **One of the best ways to ensure that your work environment is a happy place is to start with your own outlook and laugh levels.**

Start and end each day happy that you are alive!

Funny people have a positive effect on the people and environments around them.

If you are not a naturally funny person, then at least make an effort to be an optimistic work colleague who adds sunshine, as opposed to rain.

Tickle and tell! Don't keep humourous moments to yourself. Share them!

Learn to Laugh at Yourself ...

Often, we grow up to become highly respectable adults with a self-conscious distaste for being laughed at by others.

Maybe it's the fact that in our awkward teen years, our peer group can get quite carried away with cruel finger-pointing, jostling, comparing, and belittling, which results in many of us opting to quietly fly under the radar, never wanting to do or say anything even slightly humorous, so as to avoid being the centre of attention.

Some individuals get it right to maintain their sense of humour despite these painfully self-aware adolescent years.

It is very liberating to see how these individuals manage not only to laugh at themselves quite heartily but how they also readily invite others to enjoy chuckling along with them.

They do this not in a falsely humble or embarrassed fashion, but in a genuine, "No matter if I have said or done something embarrassing, I just know it's funny and I've got to laugh, so join me if you wish" manner.

Unfortunately, there is a tiny word in our English vocabulary that, despite its size, can make a huge difference in the success of our Life, Love, and Laugh Attack journeys.

This tiny, three-letter word has the power to make or break your relationships, business dealings, health and overall sense of wellness if you let it.

Let me spell it out for you:

E … G … O.

Our egos are the part of our psyches that worries about what others think about us. Our egos are closely linked to our self-image.

Nobody likes to feel inadequate; not too many people enjoy others thinking less of them either, so we spend much of our time and energy making sure that our sense of self-worth remains positive and intact.

To do this, we avoid admitting our mistakes or owning our weaknesses at all costs. We hate it if we are ever in need. We stick to the things that we are good at and avoid failure like the plague.

And heaven forbid if anyone asks us to *laugh* at ourselves!

We humans prefer to keep our egos strong, but strong egos get in the way of healthy doses of humility.

Les Brown suggests that EGO stands for "Edge God Out."

Our egos leave no space for anything in our lives bigger than what we know, see, or understand.

Humility is needed to keep us grounded enough to appreciate both the life we are living and the people who share our life journey with us.

We get separated from our true significance and size in this world if we let go of humility.

The problem with our egos, says Wayne Dyer in his DVD, *The Power of Intention,* is that they are the cause of many of our current problems, and unlike an appendectomy for an unhealthy appendix, we cannot check into the hospital to have them removed by an "ego-ectomy."

This means we actually have to work on them.

You will know you have an ego problem if you:

- cannot apologize (i.e., you hate being wrong);
- won't ask for directions;
- pretend to be a know-it-all in the office;
- refuse to listen to your GP's advice because *you* know better;
- cannot ask for help when in need of it;
- cannot delegate;
- don't trust others easily;
- are a perfectionist;
- cannot laugh at yourself or your life circumstances.

Do you recognize yourself in the list above?

Could you do better with taking yourself less seriously?

My good friend and coach, Sandy Griffin, has had her fair share of challenges in life.

Somehow, she has not only managed to retain her amazing sense of humour through it all, she has also learned how to pass on her contagious gift of laughter to others along the way.

I think that she is more than qualified to share with us a few pearls of wisdom on the subject of life and laughter.

Here is her encouragement to us on "Seeing Life's Mishaps as Stories."

Sandy Speaks

When you trip and fall, what is the first thing you do? If you are like 90 percent of most people, you look around to see if anyone saw the fall. *Then* you look down at your bleeding knee and give it attention.

We are so afraid of looking imperfect! I have news for you. We are all "perfectly imperfect." Once we accept that fact, even embrace it, our imperfect selves start to enjoy life more and actually look forward to life's mishaps.

Years ago I developed the attitude that "if you are going to laugh at something tomorrow, or even six months from now, then why wait?"

I have three wonderful daughters who have learned how to embrace life's misfortunes and laugh when the rest of the world is embarrassed at making human mistakes.

Weddings, minor car accidents, airport terminals, family gatherings—these are all places to get great material for storytelling.

Can everyone be a great storyteller? Only if they are telling their own stories!

Think of the weddings you have attended. What do you recount to your friends or families after the day's events?

Is it the tale of the flower girl who tripped on the way up the aisle, emptying her flower petals in one colourful heap, or of the ring bearer who had a temper tantrum at the altar?

What about the moment that the three-tiered wedding cake toppled over or how the bride's dress ripped when someone stepped on it?

It is the mishaps, the unexpected things, that make this special day *your* special day. These are the things that you are going to laugh about in the years to come. So why wait?

Teach yourself to "play your mishaps forward" and imagine the story they are going to become. Then remember the details. Now you are a storyteller, and an entertaining one at that!

I was at Walmart last Christmas season, leafing through a magazine before I began my Christmas and grocery shopping. As I licked my thumb to turn the page, I unknowingly licked the lime green gum I had been chewing onto my finger. This then stuck to the page. As I turned the page, too late I watched as the gum went flying—right onto the back of a lady's beautiful tweed coat!

I had two choices: I could either leave quietly or I could confess to the lady my embarrassing moment. I chose the latter. As I peeled the gum off the woman's coat, she did not even come close to cracking a smile.

I finished removing the gum, apologized profusely, and then left the store, without doing any of my shopping.

Why? Because I was embarrassed? No, I could not wait to call my sister and tell her about this funny moment. We laughed so hard that people were staring at me as tears rolled down my cheeks.

Life's mishaps. We cannot predict when they will happen, but when they do, we have the option to allow them to ruin our day or evening or to laugh and enjoy the story that they are going to become.

When you begin to tell your stories to others, it will give them permission to share the funny things that they do.

What you will find is that you will start to look forward to the mishaps that occur in your everyday life because they are now a celebration, rather than a sign of being imperfect.

I was driving from my home to my daughter's house in another state, about six hours away. As I got two blocks from her house, I decided to give my car a clean and turned into an automatic car wash.

While relaxing in my seat during the car wash cycle, I remembered that I had stopped at McDonald's for lunch and that the sack was still in the vehicle, filling it with its greasy odor.

So I decided to let some fresh air in to get rid of the smell.

Did I? Oh yes! I opened all of the windows with the automatic opener, forgetting where I was and that the water and soap were blasting at full pressure all around me.

By the time I got the windows rolled back up, I was dripping with water and soap suds. I was shocked as I felt the laughter erupt from my stomach. By the time I reached my daughter's house, I was laughing so hard, she was not sure what had happened as I gasped up to her front door.

Mistakes are just another opportunity to laugh and allow oneself to be "imperfectly perfect."

Let yourself enjoy life and life's accidents. Become the storyteller locked away inside of you. And let the laughter begin!

My Rainbow Nation

One of the strengths of the country in which I live and love, South Africa, is the ability that its people have to laugh and poke fun at themselves.

We call ourselves the "Rainbow Nation"—and for good reason. Our *eleven* official languages cater to a diversity of ethnic groups who live on South African soil and call it home.

As you travel through this beautiful country, you will encounter the smiling faces of many different peoples and a broad range of cultures, traditions, foods, clothes, preferences, and languages.

It is not always easy juggling all of this diversity.

Sometimes we just don't see eye to eye with our neighbors. Sometimes things can get *very* heated amongst us, and we can feel the tension levels rising considerably.

So we laugh!

Psychologists call this the Relief Theory of laughter: South Africans are accustomed to coping with the ever-present reality and threat of poverty, crime, political, and educational uncertainties, racism, HIV-AIDS, etc.

We know how to smile.

We recognize that a mouthful of laughter makes the tension levels go down.

We appreciate our comedians who remind us in their stand-up shows and comic books that it actually pays off in the long run to take ourselves less seriously and to let out a dry snort or two each day concerning social, political, and economic affairs.

Even our advertising on television leans towards being witty and clever, because we know that laughter brings us needed relief.

Don't get me wrong; we South Africans *can* be very proud and obstinate at times, but we do know the value of taking a few good-natured blows to our egos.

It is time to let go of your "reputation" and to embrace being authentically you!

Why don't you send your demanding ego on a one-way ticket out of here?

Why don't you pack it onto a rubber dinghy for a final voyage into the perfect comedy storm?

Conclusion: Over to You

So now we know that:

- there are *major* health benefits to having an active laugh life;
- learning to laugh with our loved ones and with the people we rub shoulders with on a daily basis has the power to mend and strengthen our relationships;
- there is no time like the present to develop a sense of humour;
- as we turn our embarrassing moments or life's mishaps into great stories, we become entertaining narrators, and our egos get delivered a healthy blow.

> **There is a Chinese proverb that says, "Blessed are those who can laugh at themselves. They shall never cease to be entertained."**

To laugh is to live and to have *quality of life,* irrespective of life's storms and unexpected challenges.

Take action. Learn to laugh.

Tell your hilarious stories—share a **Funny Five**. Don't forget to introduce a **Happy Humour Hour** at work.

Have as many moments of mirth each day as you can with friends, loved ones, work colleagues, and even complete strangers. (Those are oftentimes the best!)

Share your stories with me. I love a good laugh myself!

Tell me how your life has changed because you chose to take the *Laugh Attack Challenge.*

THE LIFE, LOVE & LAUGH ATTACK CHALLENGE

Starting a Mentor Movement

"When the end comes for you, let it find you conquering a new mountain and not sliding down an old one!"

—Jim Rohn

We can learn much from people merely by spending time in their presence.

Think of young sons who tinker around alongside their fathers under the hood of their cars, daughters who sit and watch their moms cook or bake in the kitchen, or younger siblings who tag around behind older ones to figure out what the next phase of development is all about.

As life is simply shared in this way; knowledge and skills get informally transferred from father to son, mother to daughter, and sibling to sibling, oftentimes with very little actually needing to be said.

This transference of skills and knowledge is also found in more formalized settings.

Take, for example, most major team sports, where new, energetic, and enthusiastic team members are coached by the side's older and more experienced players. They may no longer have the same speed and strength as some of these younger newbies, but they are still crucial to the team's make-up because of their know-how.

This process of accessing the insights of individuals a few steps ahead of us on life's journey is often referred to as *mentoring*.

What Is a Mentor?

A mentor is someone who epitomizes living the life you long to live—whether it is in the area of health and fitness, wealth, relationships, or spirituality—and whose influence you intentionally seek out and accept because you regard the person to be an individual of good counsel.

Ideally, a mentor will be able to assist you in looking at life objectively and honestly enough to figure out why you may not be achieving the desired results from your behavior or actions.

As writer H. Jackson Brown, Jr. said, "Talent without discipline is like an octopus on roller skates. There's plenty of movement, but you never know if it's going to be forward, backwards or sideways."

A good mentor will help introduce *discipline* into the areas of your life that need it, and in doing so, will help you establish a clearer vision and direction for your life.

> **At times, a mentor will believe in you more than you are able to and will loan you this belief until you have adequately found your own "life legs."**

I love the example from the 1994 animated movie, *The Lion King*, which tells the story of Simba, a young lion cub who struggles to believe in his worth and destiny after his evil uncle, Scar, frames him for the death of his father, the king, Mufasa.

Riddled with guilt over what he believes he has done, the young Simba runs away from his homelands and lives an exiled life with the unlikely friends that he makes along the way.

Mufasa's wise and elderly friend and counselor, Rafiki, eventually seeks Simba out when he is an adult lion to urge him to return to the pride lands and to challenge his evil uncle for the stolen title of king.

This encounter with Rafiki serves as a catalyst for Simba to awaken his longing for his destiny. At this point, the spirit of his dead father steps in.

Mufasa encourages the young lion, as he grapples with feelings of shame and uncertainty about his worth, to recognize that he is more than he has allowed himself to become. Simba's hope for his future lies in his ability to overcome his self doubt and embrace his true identity.

Both Rafiki and Mufasa know this to be true and long for Simba to see and realize it for himself.

Sometimes, we need Rafikis or Mufasas of our very own to tell us what we are capable of when we are struggling to see or believe it.

> **Sometimes we need an available friend who has gone on before us, whose hindsight can become *our* foresight.**

My Mentoring Momentum

According to Paul Martinelli, we can never underestimate the power of access, influence, and connection we can acquire through an accountable relationship with a mentor.

The first step that I took to gain momentum in my own mentoring relationships was to choose a life coach for myself.

Sandy Griffin helped me kick-start my Life Attack in the right direction by holding me accountable to my commitments.

Later, I increased my team of mentors by joining Les Brown and Paul Martinelli on their Empowerment Mentoring Programme. This programme brings together an incredible group of people for a two-day conference in Florida. Here, Les and Paul hunker right down to eye level with participants and help them work out some of the nitty-gritties of their life journeys.

Paul then brought to my attention the new John C. Maxwell's leadership Certification program that John and his team had developed for individuals wanting to expand their leadership horizons. John is the number 1 Leadership Guru and one of the best researched individuals contributing to the field of leadership and development in the world at present. There was no way that I was going to let this opportunity to rub shoulders with him pass me by! I joined Maxwell's Founders Circle in March of 2011 and began the life changing process of becoming an accredited John C Maxwell Speaker, Coach and Trainer. What a privilege to visit with John and his family at their beautiful home in Florida and be permitted to train individuals and businesses alike on his programs!

For those wanting to get their hands on some very substantial and sound leadership development material, I highly recommend this mentorship program. It has made a huge difference in helping me live out my own life purpose. Please contact me for more details on this program and I will share more of my journey with pleasure.

Starting a Mentor Movement

Finding yourself a mentor or mentorship programme is one of the last steps that I encourage you to take on your Life, Love and Laugh Attack voyage.

Within the next ninety days, I challenge you to both *find* yourself a mentor and *become* a mentor to someone else.

Will you join me in starting a mentor movement?

1. **Find yourself a mentor.**

Do you already have a potential mentor in mind?

Is there an individual ahead of you on life's journey who is notably committed to living, loving, and laughing well?

Would you benefit from deliberately setting aside time to spend with this person, in order to listen to their life stories and experiences, and to glean from them lessons learned and wisdom gained over the years?

This you can use as leverage for your own life journey.

Invite and pay for them to join you for lunch, ask them a pertinent question, and sit back and *really* take note of their perspectives on living, loving, and laughing.

You can then begin the process of adapting what seems fit from these encounters into your own life.

2. **Become a mentor to at least one other person in your sphere of influence.**

> **My experience is that there are always people who are looking for someone to mentor them through a particular age and stage of their life.**

Your life experiences can serve to encourage others on their own journey!

My experience is that we grow *exponentially* when we focus on giving of ourselves to others in this way; we learn alongside those we teach and with whom we share life.
So I encourage you to challenge and stimulate growth in your own person by giving away what you have already received.

Whom do you mentor?

My experience has been that the people who need mentoring arrive on the scene of our lives just in time for us to add value to their journeys.

Such individuals could be working in your profession and might need your qualified input for a season; others might be a few paces behind you in life development and could do with some encouragement and counsel.

Our role is to keep our eyes open to identify these individuals as they enter our orbit.

On occasion, people might enter your life whose age and stage might not be ideal to receive mentoring from you.

People who feel they already have all the answers will soon frustrate you in the mentoring relationship, so it's best to gently steer them on their way.

Do the same to the person who just wants to take and take and take from you; this type of relationship leaves you drained of needed energy and enthusiasm for future mentoring relationships.

Instead, be on the lookout for people who are hungry to grow and learn from you, who are responsible and adult enough to *own* their Life Attack journeys, and who you feel could benefit from what you already know.

THE LIFE, LOVE & LAUGH ATTACK CHALLENGE

Conclusion

"I've never had so much fun as I'm going to have tomorrow!"
—Dennis the Menace

Can you feel the winds of change beginning to blow through your Life Boat sails?

Is the horizon ahead of you starting to take a more adventurous shape?

Have you dusted off your Life Attack Challenge tools, asked pertinent questions about your *passion,* taken the time to write down your *vision* and daily *goals* needed to fulfill it, taking *action* where needed to pursue your dreams, harnessed your *thought life* to work on your behalf instead of letting it sink you, and found a *mentor or life coach* to keep you accountable on the journey?

Let me stop you right there. If you have read this book and not taken the time to actually discover your passion and write down a purpose statement, *now* is that time.

Have you begun to challenge some of the obstructive critters loafing on your Life Boat - critters like self-doubt, fear, confusion, dreamlessness, apathy, and boredom, selfish ambition, lovelessness, respectability, and somberness?

Have you laughed a whole lot more of late, and is your Life Boat trading well in matters of the heart?

If need be, go back and revisit those sections of the book that still need proper application in your life, remembering that this Life Attack journey is more of a *lifestyle* than a short trip around a harbor.[46]

There is not much left for me to say other than to wish you well on your Life, Love and Laugh Attack journey.

If you see me out on life's ocean, please take the time to shout, "Ahoy!" and share with me your Life, Love, and Laugh Attack story.

46 We all like quick fixes. Quick fixes do not stick. A *purposeful* change in thinking, decision-making, and behaviour, on the other hand, will.